If you are expecting this book to be a Christian version of Aladdin's magic lamp, one where you rub things a certain way and recite some incantations which will somehow manipulate God into giving you whatever your flesh craves, this book is not for you. If that kind of ear tickling is your cup of tea, close this book, put it down, and walk away. You won't like what you find here.

However, if you are serious about walking with God wherever that takes you, being led by the Spirit, and allowing Him to transform you by the renewing of your mind through God's Word and committing to a lifestyle of prayer, buy this book, devour its contents, and practice what you have discovered.

Your life will be vastly enriched.

Ask & You *Shall* Receive!

Maximize the Effectiveness of Your Prayer Life

by

Mark Stevens Willis, PhD

WORD & SPIRIT
PUBLISHING
www.wordandspiritpublishing.com

Published by
Word & Spirit Publishing
PO Box 701403 • Tulsa, OK 74170
wordandspiritpublishing.com

ISBN: 978-1-685730-13-0

Printed in the United States of America

Table of Contents

Dedication

This book is written to the glory of Daddy God,
the lordship of Jesus the Messiah,
the power of the Holy Spirit,
the triumph of His Church over the gates of Hell
and the prayer warriors who fight to make that happen.

This book is dedicated to you, the reader.
You are not reading this by accident!

Acknowledgements

Far too many people and organizations have spoken into my life over the last 50 years to credit them all here, so I'll have to limit myself to hitting the high points.

My beautiful and godly wife Tess, called by God to my side from over 6200 miles away in the Philippines, tops that list. She is the undisputed queen of my heart. That tired old cliché of "she makes me a better person" doesn't begin to cover the ways God has used her to help me turn into the man of God I am today. A complete description of her wonderfulness would require yet another book, so you'll just have to trust me on this!

I would also like to express my gratitude to The Navigators and Youth With A Mission. Each had a tremendous impact on my early spiritual life. The principles I learned from these organizations remain with me to this day and are integral to the foundation of who I am as a believer and a minister.

Next would be the following:

- Dr. Douglas Wingate, President of Life Christian University (my alma mater and former employer) who was an awesome boss, faithful friend, and anointed minister and educator.

- The late John Little, a fellow GI who led me to Christ, later graduated from seminary after his enlistment was over, and then re-enlisted to become an Army chaplain. RIP, my friend!

- Jim Albert, the then-Air Force sergeant who discipled me as a new believer. Whenever we hit a controversial doctrinal topic and I would ask his opinion on the matter, his consistent response was, "What does the Word say?" I will be forever grateful for his advice!

- Pastor William Burgess, who discipled me as a minister during the early 1990s. Through him, I developed a pastor's heart — an entirely different kettle of fish than a pastor's calling — and witnessed first-hand the compassion of Christ in action. He remains one of my closest friends and confidants to this day.

- Pastors David and Frances Oberg who pastor Faith Alive Christian Center in Reno, Nevada. David has always been an example and inspiration to me through his incredible work ethic and personal integrity in the face of persecution. He and Fran have also been there for me during some really dark days in my life. Without their intervention, I would most likely be living in a cardboard box under a bridge somewhere.

- Pastor Virgil Stokes, founder and pastor of Faith Christian Fellowship of Tucson. Several of the concepts in this book have his excellent teaching in their DNA.

- Another former pastor, Ron Merrell, who inspires me with his incredible messages and encourages me with his friendship.

- Friends not already mentioned: John & Stacey Foster, Pete & Deb Parise, and Barry Martin, all of whom have faithfully been there for me through the good times and the bad.

- Finally, my gifted editor, the multi-talented Gail Jean Dunkle, a fellow expatriate Texan with a heart of gold as big as our former state. She's been a huge inspiration to me for years and among all the nice things I could say about her, one thing stands head-and-shoulders above all the rest: *she's a prayer warrior* in the truest sense of the term.

Foreword

THERE ARE FRIENDS AND THEN THERE ARE friends who are powerful prayer warriors.

It took me about a week after joining the pastoral staff at our church to recognize that God had provided me one of those once-in-a-lifetime, fervent, faithful, prayer-warrior friends in Steve Willis. He introduced himself to me on my opening weekend, offering anything I needed, and made a specific point that he'd be praying for me as I got my feet settled in our new community.

Steve followed up the next weekend with another warm greeting and confirmation that he'd been praying about my first week in town. I knew then his words and his prayers were more than just a gracious welcome. Now after over 6 years of friendship, I'm blessed to have had a front row seat to someone who loves God and loves people with everything he's got — so much so that he prays continually!

His passion for prayer was born out of seasons of strong adversity and deep study of God's Word. As a result, Steve is instrumental in keeping prayer a priority in our church, helping others understand what prayer is and how to do it, as well as praying continually for those in need in our community. Indeed, I am not the only one in our church blessed by his friendship and prayers.

Now this book is an opportunity for you to be blessed in a similar way. You'll find answers to questions you've always had about the Scriptures, God's character, and prayer — all in plain, understandable language. You'll be provoked to do your own study and rethink areas that are often debated in theological circles. Most importantly, you'll press deeper into a relationship with the Living God.

Knowing Steve, that's his heart for you as you read this book. Your relationship with Jesus was meant to be intimate and thriving and powerful. A prayer life conformed to God's Word is crucial in cultivating your relationship with Jesus, your growing into the person He designed you to be, and you playing your part in advancing God's Kingdom here on earth.

So start reading! And please know I'll be praying for you as you read.

Just like my friend Steve taught me.

Pastor Ron Merrell
Teaching Pastor
Connection Pointe Church
Indianapolis, Indiana

Preface

I'M A BORN-FROM-ABOVE FOLLOWER OF Jesus Christ. I'm also one of the least religious people you will ever meet. What do I mean by this? *I'm a radical.*

I stand apart from most of the classic stereotypes — within and without Christendom — of what most folks assume a Christ-follower is and should be, believe and not believe (apart from the core doctrines of Christianity, that is), and stand for or against in the marketplace of ideas and pop culture.

Jesus the Radical is my Lord and example. He stood in loving opposition to everything the culture, society, and governmental/religious establishments of His day deemed normal and proper, while showing compassionate mercy to the marginalized and healing the sick and the wounded.

As a radical, I believe Christ-followers are supposed to be culturally relevant, not culturally compliant. We are called to be counter-culture revolutionaries the same way believers operated for the first 300 years of the Church's existence. Jesus calls us to be salt and light, not chameleons. We're supposed to be transforming our societies and cultures by our loving witness, not conforming to it through a misguided craving for social respectability.

I wrote this book to address two pandemic problems within the American church today:

1. Rampant prayerlessness, and;
2. What I believe to be its primary causes: the encroachment of man's religion into Christian theology and pervasive scriptural illiteracy within the Body of Christ.

This spiritually deadly mash-up of corrupted doctrines and the resulting apathetic prayer behavior exhibited by most American Christians has opened wide the door for the secularization of the United States and the rest of Western Civilization.

I am convinced the commandments, doctrines, and traditions of men have so repelled the unsaved and marginally churched in this nation that they have thrown away the Truth-of-the-Gospel baby with the religious-nonsense-of-men bath water. They cannot see the real Jesus because our religious baggage is obscuring their vision of the *only* Way, the *only* Truth, and the *only* Life.

Until and unless we ruthlessly root out man's religion and its shame-based, performance-oriented mentality from our beliefs and return to the purity of the Word, the love of God, our freedom in Christ, and the power of the Holy Spirit, our country's devolution into religious, political, and economic chaos will continue unabated.

Why?

Because our salt has become tasteless and we have hidden our light under a traditions-of-men bushel.

The disastrous consequences of all this are being seen throughout our post-modern society. We've lost the moral compass our nation was founded upon. This has opened the door wide for attacks of the enemy as witnessed by 9/11, the Boston Marathon bombing, mass shootings, frequent riots, daily hate crimes, rapidly growing anti-Semitism, persecution of Christians and Jews, and the almost-daily ethical/moral failures of our governmental and church leaders.

Our country appears to be rapidly devolving into a diseased, empty husk of its former self.

Despite the valiant efforts of transient godly leaders, our country flounders about on the world stage while locked in a no-holds-barred cold-civil-war between the powers of darkness and the Kingdom of God battling for the soul of America. Satan dominates both mass and social media as well as pop culture to so completely it appears to be a hopeless battle already all but lost.

The entire world is suffering for it.

That's the bad news.

Our Good News is this:

- *Jesus is alive and well.* He is still on His throne. No one, repeat no one, can unseat Him. He remains — and always will be — King of Kings and Lord of Lords.
- Our Heavenly Father is faithful to His Word. He is redemptive in His intentions/purposes. He is relentless in His lovingkindness toward us as individuals, as well as our wayward nation, no matter how far we have strayed.
- He hears the petitions of bold, fervent, and persistent prayer warriors who are crazy enough to believe He will answer them in the affirmative. He not only hears, but actually delivers what He has clearly promised:

  …if My people who are called by My name will humble themselves, and pray and seek My face, and turn from their wicked ways, then I will hear from heaven, and will forgive their sin and heal their land. — 2 Chronicles 7:14

- Our weapons are supremely powerful in pulling down strongholds and anything else exalting itself against the knowledge of God.

- God's grace is more than sufficient for us to not only endure, but prevail!

Developing the faith to pray successfully for a nation begins with our learning how to get our prayers answered for smaller stuff so we are victorious over the powers of darkness in our own lives.

This book will help you with both.

God bless you!

MSW

CHAPTER

1

Introduction to Prayer

IN THIS BOOK, I WILL BE SHARING THE scriptural precepts and principles concerning prayer I have learned and experienced personally.

Why?

So you, too, can supercharge what I hope is already a daily prayer life. My desire is for you to get to a place spiritually where you can:

> *...come boldly to the throne of grace, that we may obtain mercy and find grace to help in time of need.— Hebrews 4:16*

For such a confident approach to take place, we first need some enlightenment from the Word of God. We need this to overcome our natural fear of dealing with our holy, all-knowing Almighty God.

Let's get started!

Prayer in My Personal Walk with God

Prayer was not a top priority for me in my early Christian life. Though I had received excellent teaching on the topic, for much of that time I was far more a hearer of the Word rather than a doer. All that head-knowledge became a hard, cold reality to me just after the turn of this century.

Prior to that time, I had interacted with people claiming to be intercessors and prayer warriors, but most of them were hyper-spiritual, self-righteous, smug, doctrinally flaky, and many times just plain weird.

I wanted no part of it!

However, once prayer became a necessity for my personal survival, when, if God didn't answer my prayers, I would be homeless and sleeping under an overpass somewhere, all my excuses fell to the wayside. I became deadly serious about becoming a doer of the Word concerning prayer!

Prayer in the Church

One tragic observation I've made over my last 50 years of walking with God is that within any church of any size — be it a congregation of 200, 2,000, or 20,000 — only a tiny percentage of its members will faithfully show up for a weekly prayer meeting to pray for our nation and its leaders, their church and its leaders, and the congregation's individual prayer requests. It seems like prayer is the red-headed stepchild of the Church — we acknowledge its existence and give lip-service to its value, but refuse to commit ourselves heart and soul to it.

For a group who claims to follow Jesus, who personally both taught and exemplified a vital prayer life, we are doing an amazingly poor job of imitation!

I firmly believe this is because of a single point of failure: their pastoral staffs ignore the following principle:

> *Whatever behavior shepherds value highly enough to repeatedly teach on from the pulpit, announce from the platform, and personally show up for, their sheep will participate in it. Flocks are led, not commanded or driven.*

It's the old leadership maxim that people will only follow where you, as a leader, are willing to go. Being "too busy" or "I've delegated this" are not valid excuses — it simply means your ministerial priorities are out of whack and desperately need adjustment.

Church leaders reading this, *selah!*

The Church desperately needs to see its leaders demonstrating prayer so they will understand the hows and the whys and the wherefores of doing it. Much of what we learn about prayer is caught, not taught, though teaching certainly has value or I wouldn't have written this book!

Should God ever call me to lead a congregation, there will always be a weekly prayer meeting. My wife and I will always show up for it unless it is impossible due to personal tragedy, serious illness, or being out of town. Every bulletin will list it. Every announcement from the platform at every service will include it. Prayer will frequently recur as a sermon topic. I will allow no other church events to preempt it in the activities schedule. As Jesus declared when He drove out the money-changers from the temple, *"My house shall be a house of prayer!"*

The 2 Most Important Things About Prayer

The most important thing about prayer is we are doing it!

If we are not fluent or knowledgeable at first, the Holy Spirit can educate and adjust us over time with additional insights into and correction from His Word. But we should never, ever allow our ignorance or inexperience to be an excuse for not praying!

The second-most important thing is prayer is not about us, but is about Him. Only our corrupt flesh and Satan's hordes are sitting on the sidelines, awarding points for technical excellence and artistic merit.

God doesn't care one iota about your eloquence/sophistication of speech, the size of your vocabulary, your ability to quote Scripture verbatim or your ability — or lack thereof — to pray in King James English.

What He does demand from us?

Honesty and humility.

Why these two?

- No relationship with anyone — especially the Almighty — can succeed apart from honesty, and;
- We must humbly come to Him by His grace alone with zero sense of entitlement based on our filthy-rags righteousness and/or dead religious works.

But I'm so Unworthy!

Aren't we all? Deal with it!

Our worthiness to "boldly come to the throne of grace" is only by God's grace expressed through Jesus' finished work of the Cross — and *nothing* else! We absolutely cannot add to or detract from His imparted righteousness as described by the Apostle Paul:

> *For He (God the Father) made Him (Jesus) who knew no sin to be sin for us, that we might become the righteousness of God in Him (Jesus). — 2 Corinthians 5:21 (parentheses mine)*

In theological circles, this is called "The Great Exchange." Sinless Jesus became our sin on the cross, so we sinners would become righteous with His righteousness. That supernatural event takes place in the spirit the very moment any person confesses Jesus as Lord and believes God raised Him from the dead (Romans 10:9-10).

It is absolutely crucial we Christ-followers have complete assurance of our salvation. If we are not thoroughly convinced we have a God-given right to be before His throne of grace, we will not go boldly, if at all, ever. The fastest way to kill your prayer life is thinking your performance — or lack thereof — has anything to do with the equation!

No Recipes!

Prayer is not about recipes or formulæ because such things are intrinsic to man's religion, whereas God is all about relationships.

Truth be told, prayers using recipes and formulæ are a form of sorcery. Sorcery is any human practice where our saying the "correct" words while performing the "correct" rituals in a "correct" order, and behaving in a "correct" manner will produce a desired supernatural blessing. It's all about manipulation and control.

The bottom line to this bogus religious economy is if we speak and behave properly, we will receive whatever we desire from God because He will owe us for our obedience. This is completely alien to the message of Christ.

The only formula in play here is this:

> *Grace + Truth + Time = Spiritual Growth*
> *— How People Grow (Drs. Henry Cloud & John Townsend)*

We grow spiritually whenever we:

- Apply God's truth
- By God's grace
- In the context of God's people
- Over a time-frame of God's choosing.

Our problems start when we omit one of these from the equation or over-emphasize one of them at the expense of the other two. For example:

> ***We grow when we apply God's truth by God's grace in the context of God's people over a time-frame of God's choosing.***

- If we over-emphasize grace, we end up with "greasy grace," a kind of *laissez-aller* or "anything goes" mentality. Such an unscriptural mind-set fails to hold us accountable for our behavior.
- If we base things on truth alone, we will indeed have the required accountability. However, when we exclude grace, we end up with legalism, which is equally unscriptural.

We are relational beings created in the image and likeness of a relational God. We mature spiritually through our relationships with Him and our brothers and sisters in Christ. If we try to fly solo, we will ultimately fail because Christianity is a team sport. The concept of spiritual Lone Rangers cannot be found anywhere in the New Testament.

If we omit time from the equation, we will experience continual frustration. There is no such thing as "add-water-and-stir" Christianity. God uses time to develop our character, which, by the way, is His #2 priority (#1 is an intimate personal relationship).

If God will favorably respond to the faith of an untrained child, he will respond to you with equal favor! That being said, there are principles concerning prayer in God's Word that — when we apply them — put us in a far better position to receive answers to our prayers. Those principles will be our topics of discussion in the following chapters.

Prayer is a growth process. No one has "arrived!" We will face faith challenges and be praying for answers to them for the rest of our time on this earth. Get used to the idea! As Navy SEALs are given to say, "The only easy day was yesterday" Our faith challenges only get bigger and more difficult over time.

That's the bad news.

The Good News is God's grace is always more than enough to get us through them all victoriously! (2 Corinthians 11:9a)

CHAPTER

2

Prayer Defined

THE HEART OF ALL PRAYER IS THIS: it is a conversation between a disciple of the Lord Jesus Christ and the One True God. Access to our Father God is only through Jesus' blood and His finished work of the Cross. How do we know this? Because Jesus Himself said it:

> *Jesus said to him, "I am the way, the truth, and the life. No one comes to the Father except through Me. —John 14:7*

Facts About Prayer

- Prayer is singularly personal, incredibly intimate, and organic to a vital relationship with God.
- Prayer — along with God's Word — is the spiritual lifeblood of all believers. *Accept no substitutes because they are all counterfeits!*
- Prayer aligns us with the heart of God over time. We progressively care more and more about what He cares about, we

conform our priorities with His, we align our thought processes with His thoughts, and His desires become ours.

- Prayer invites the God of the Universe to intervene in the affairs of mankind. The Bible records many accounts of God's people praying to Him and how He then changed the course of a person's or nation's history in response to those prayers.

- Jesus constantly modeled prayer — in priority, principle, and practice — for His disciples and, in turn, for us.

- The Bible contains guidelines for effective prayer and promises for those who do pray.

- Prayer is described in the Bible as incense in the presence of God:

> *Now when He had taken the scroll, the four living creatures and the twenty-four elders fell down before the Lamb, each having a harp, and golden bowls full of incense, which are the prayers of the saints." — Revelation 5:8*

Generally speaking, according to Jesus in the gospels, we are supposed to pray to the Father in the name of Jesus. But there is nothing saying we cannot pray directly to Jesus or the Holy Spirit. After all, they are all one God.

Types of Prayer

Salvation

Surrendering to the lordship of Jesus Christ by grace through faith, believing that God raised Him from the dead. This is how someone receives the New Birth (John 3).

Repentance

Repenting of our sins and confessing them to God, thereby receiving His mercy and forgiveness. Repentance is an abandonment of our self-lordship (aka sin) and resubmission to the lordship of Jesus in any given area of life.

Consecration

Dedicating oneself or one's nation, church, family, or possessions to the service and glory of the Almighty.

Supplication

Asking God to:

- Do or provide something based upon promises in His Word, specifically blessing us in some form or fashion by meeting our spiritual, mental, emotional, physical, financial, or family needs
- Resolve specific difficulties or challenges we may be facing, both large and small
- Give us guidance/wisdom so we know what to say and/or do in a personal, relational, business/employment situation
- Etc., etc.

Intercession

The same as a prayer of supplication, but expressed on the behalf of other individuals and/or groups rather than ourselves.

Thanksgiving

Expressing gratitude to God for the mighty works He has done, is doing, or will be doing in our lives and/or the lives of others.

Worship

Expressing praise and worship for Who God is as well as His character and attributes

Imprecation

These are prayers calling down God's wrath upon the wicked or those who have wronged us. Such prayers are frequently found in the Psalms of David as he struggled spiritually with the attacks of his enemies.

This type of prayer, though, has been superseded by Jesus' command to:

> *"…love your enemies, bless those who curse you, do good to those who hate you, and pray for those who spitefully use you and persecute you" — Matthew 5:44*

Why? Because:

> *"…we do not wrestle against flesh and blood, but against principalities, against powers, against the rulers of the darkness of this age, against spiritual hosts of wickedness in the heavenly places." — Ephesians 6:12*

Submission & Confrontation

Prayer is simultaneously an act of humble submission and raw, naked aggression. Why do I say this?

Because we are always humbling ourselves, submitting to the lordship of Jesus Christ while using our God-given authority to aggressively confront negative circumstances and the powers of darkness, ordering them to cease and desist their evil schemes.

It is crucial these two never get mixed up in our minds. We are never to submit to adverse circumstances or the evil plans/purposes/schemes of the powers of darkness — this leads to defeat — but resist them with the Word of God while being submitted to the lordship of Jesus, which is where our authority to do so comes from.

We are never to demand anything of God — He is the Lord God, King of the Universe Who responds to our prayers of faith through His grace by honoring His Word. We never approach God with any sense of entitlement because He is absolutely not our cosmic bellhop here to wait on us hand and foot, catering to our selfish whims. We work for Him, not the other way around

Misconceptions About Prayer

Getting Our Prayers Answered Depends on How Holy or Spiritual We Are

Well, yes and no. Yes, rebellious acts and sinful attitudes will cripple our prayer life. On the other hand, we don't have to be perfect or achieve some state of enlightenment or level of holiness to have our prayers heard and answered affirmatively.

Remember, it's all by grace!

God Likes Us Better Because We Pray

Well, yes and no, again. Will we draw closer in our relationship to God by praying? *Absolutely!* But no, we cannot enhance our standing before God through prayer because, as we've already covered earlier, we are already as righteous (spotless, blameless) as we will ever be by the blood of Jesus and the finished work of the Cross — we cannot enhance or detract from what Jesus has already accomplished!

For example, my son is no less my son if he chooses to exclude me from his daily life. Such estrangement does not define our relationship, but does limit the ease and change the nature of our communications.

God Cares About Our Posture or Apparel

The historic stereotype is we must be fully clothed or in pajamas and kneel with our hands held or folded together and our head bowed either in a church or by our beds.

Actually, we can scripturally pray in any position: standing, kneeling, sitting, squatting, supine (laying down, looking upward), prone (laying down, on our faces before God), or while walking, running, swimming, or driving. Our hands can be clasped, raised to God, or stuck in our pockets, for all God cares! Our heads can be bowed, looking upward, or resting on a pillow. We can be located in a church, our homes, our cars, at work, out among nature, on city streets. We can be fully clothed, partially clothed, or buck naked.

In other words, God can — and most importantly, wants to — hear us just fine regardless of where we are, what we are doing, or how we are dressed — or undressed, for that matter!

Aloud or Silently?

Scripturally, prayer is generally spoken aloud except in those rare circumstances where we are not permitted to speak for external reasons (usually persecution of some kind). God knows our thoughts and hearts, so speaking aloud is not a requirement for Him to hear us. That being said, there are others who cannot read our thoughts and minds, specifically everyone who is *not* God.

I've found only one place in the Bible where it records an instance of silent prayer, the prayer of childless Hannah:

> *And she was in bitterness of soul, and prayed to the Lord and wept in anguish. Then she made a vow and said, "O Lord of hosts, if You will indeed look on the affliction of Your maidservant and remember me, and not forget Your maidservant, but will give Your maidservant a male child, then I will give him*

> *to the Lord all the days of his life, and no razor shall come upon his head." And it happened, as she continued praying before the Lord, that Eli watched her mouth. Now Hannah spoke in her heart; only her lips moved, but her voice was not heard. Therefore Eli thought she was drunk. — 1 Samuel 1:10-13*

The answer to that prayer was the book's namesake, the prophet Samuel. But that is by far the exception rather than the rule throughout the Scriptures.

In my opinion, the modern "silent prayer" or "silent request" are devices used by:

- The immature to disguise their embarrassment over the issue needing prayer or over their feelings of inadequacy to pray aloud in the presence of others, or;
- Those who are trying to hide their sin(s) and are concealing them to avoid correction (more on this in Group #3 below).

Group #1: Ourselves

Our words are a powerful creative force in this earth and it is our words which give our thoughts substance in our own minds. Bringing concepts into mental clarity requires putting them into words organized into sentences which can then be understood by ourselves and others. When we pray aloud, we are bringing our disjointed thoughts and desires into focus and drawing a line in the sand, so to speak, indicating what we are making a stand on spiritually in our own minds.

Please note how even in the account of Hannah's silent prayer just referenced, she was actually moving her lips, mouthing the words of her prayer, rather than kneeling there thinking them.

Group #2: Satan & Demons

Our psychopathic enemy needs to know we and the persons for whom we pray are not going to be doormats for his schemes. While his servants can whisper thoughts into our spiritual ears, none of them can read our minds, so we cannot command Satan's crew to leave or stop doing something using our thoughts alone.

This is a major problem for many Christians who do not realize this. They persist in trying to resist temptation or overcome mental torment by "thinking them away." If we look at Jesus' example, nowhere in the Gospels did he "think" the powers of darkness away from Himself or others. He spoke to them, commanding them to leave, as do we!

Group #3: Those Who We Want to Agree With Us in Prayer

A prayer of agreement is quite powerful because Jesus Himself said:

> *Again I say to you that if two of you agree on earth concerning anything that they ask, it will be done for them by My Father in heaven. For where two or three are gathered together in My name, I am there in the midst of them. — Matthew 18:19-20*

And Solomon said:

> *Though one may be overpowered by another, two can withstand him. — Ecclesiastes 3:12*

Agreement is the mechanism undergirding the practices of establishing prayer chains and conducting prayer meetings, when many people are praying in agreement, joining their faith in one accord as they pray to the Father over one or more matters. More than a few major moves of God in the earth have been brought to pass through such groups!

However, we cannot agree with someone unless we know what we are agreeing to. This produces accountability, ensuring the desires expressed and the prayers spoken are righteous.

Case in point: a famous evangelist was working his way down a line of people who had responded to an altar call at one of his services, laying hands upon them and praying for each one individually. When he came to one man, the man stated that he had a silent request. The evangelist informed him that there was no way he was going to pray in agreement with a silent request — he had to know what he was agreeing to.

After a few moments of hesitation, the man blurted out how he was in love with a woman who was not his wife and he wanted the evangelist to agree with his prayer that God would kill his wife so he could marry the other woman.

Obviously, the evangelist refused to pray in agreement with such a sinful and unscriptural desire!

Why Do We Pray?

Now that we've defined what prayer is and isn't, let's spend some time answering that question.

The Divine Imperative

First and foremost: *we are commanded to pray.* Among other verses along those lines, we read the following passages in two of Paul's epistles:

> *Continue earnestly in prayer, being vigilant in it with thanksgiving, — Colossians 4:2*
>
> *Rejoice always, pray without ceasing, in everything give thanks; for this is the will of God in Christ Jesus for you.*
> *— 1 Thessalonians 5:16–18*

Please note both references are in the imperative voice, ergo they are commands, not suggestions. Since we are thus commanded to pray, prayerlessness on our part is indeed sin.

If you find yourself in such a state as you're reading this, I'm not saying these things to shame or guilt you into praying. Guilt and shame are terrible motivators and God never uses them.

I am saying this so you will see there is something terribly amiss with your walk with God which desperately needs correction. What I pray you do with this insight is repent, ask His forgiveness, and ask Him to help you correct this so you will have the vital prayer life God desires and the Bible portrays for all believers.

Exercising Spiritual Authority

As we will explore in much greater detail in Chapter 6, whenever we pray, we are exercising our God-given authority over His earth and what happens in it, as well as over the powers of darkness.

Believers who will boldly come to the throne of grace and plead the promises of God for our corrupt cesspit of a world can arrest the plans and purposes of our enemy, the psychopath god of this world, Satan. This concept is exemplified in the Book of James:

> *But He gives more grace. Therefore He says: 'God resists the proud, But gives grace to the humble.' Therefore submit to God. Resist the devil and he will flee from you. —James 4:6-7*

How do we resist him? Through prayer, standing in the authority God has given us over him, his followers, and his works.

Effective Prayer is Based Upon Accurate Revelation

Our prayers have their foundation in an accurate revelation of Who God is, who we are, how He relates to us, and how He wants us to relate to Him. What I mean by this is our knowledge of these things is rooted and grounded in accurate knowledge of God's Word rather than the lies of man's religion.

Who Is God?

Faithful: He can always be depended upon to keep His Word.

True: He never lies or promises something He will not do.

Loving: He cares for us beyond our ability to imagine.

Kind: He actively desires to help us.

Generous: He is not stingy and assists us beyond the minimum needed to get by.

Merciful: He does not hold our past mistakes against us as an excuse to not answer our prayers.

Gracious: He extends infinite, unmerited favor towards us.

Willing: He is actively desiring — and looking for ways — to help us.

Available: He is always available at anytime of the day or night. He is never too busy and our concerns are never too insignificant for His attention.

Impartial: He keeps all His promises to all his children, not merely the ones we consider to be over-achievers.

Who Are We?

Beloved, not barely tolerated

Precious, valuable, and treasured, not worthless

Significant, not inconsequential or expendable

Safe, not threatened or endangered

How Are We Related?

- We are the righteousness of God in Christ, spotless and without blemish.
- We are seated with Jesus in heavenly places.
- We have been given authority over the powers of darkness.

- We have been given authority over the power of sin.
- We have been given everything that pertains to life and godliness.
- We possess His exceedingly great and precious promises.
- We have been adopted as sons and daughters of the King.
- We can boldly come before the throne of grace to seek help and grace in time of need.
- Our inheritance is guaranteed by the indwelling of the Holy Spirit.
- We have been brought near to God by the blood of Christ.
- We are reconciled to God.
- We have access by one Spirit to the Father.
- We are no longer strangers and foreigners, but fellow citizens with the saints in the household of God.

Obviously, these things are a whole different kettle of fish than what we find in man's religion!

Before we dig further into the topic of prayer, we first need to establish some crucial foundational principles upon which we can build a successful prayer life. This we will do in the next several chapters.

CHAPTER

3

Humility: Part 1

BEFORE WE PROCEED FURTHER, WE MUST first explore the crucial topic of humility in far greater depth. This issue is way too foundational to a successful prayer life to merely brush past it with the cursory mention I gave it in Chapter 1.

Even casual Bible-readers can quickly detect God's high regard for the humble. Tragically, many proclaiming themselves "Christian" these days appear to have either glossed over or mentally redacted those passages entirely.

This is especially evident among so-called Word of Faith believers. I can legitimately make that call because: 1) I are one, and; 2) I used to exhibit such an attitude in spades (more on that later).

Before we get started, though, the great danger inherent to writing about humility is being perceived as proclaiming the equivalent of *"Humility & How I Achieved It"* which of course completely negates everything being said.

Let me hasten to assure you I have not "arrived" at this virtue — I'm still very much a work-in-progress a full 20 years after my serious journey towards humility first began. If you have any trouble accepting my claim at face value, simply ask my wife who can and will gladly provide abundant and compelling supporting evidence!

So I guess you could subtitle this chapter *"A Lesson on Humility From One Who Battles Pride."*

Our Reaction to Arrogance Echoes God's

Have you ever encountered a rebellious teenager who has "copped a 'tude" and mouthed off at you? If you haven't yet, simply wait long enough and you absolutely will (back in my childhood, drastic and painful retribution quickly followed. Your mileage may vary)! Since we are created in the likeness and image of God (Genesis 2), why would we think God feels any differently?

Now imagine the infinite patience, mercy, and grace required to deal with literally billions of clueless, rebellious teenagers all dancing around with their spiritual fingers stuck tightly in their ears, shouting, "La, la, la, la!" You now have a faint glimpse of what our loving Creator handles second-by-second with mankind.

Mind-boggling, isn't it!

Misconceptions About Humility

Misconception #1: Humble = Worthless

One of the many disservices man's religion has inflicted upon us is its conflation of humility with worthlessness.

This is absolutely antithetical to the Bible, *period.*

All human beings have inherent value and significance simply by existing because The Almighty has clearly and unequivocally declared it so by word and action. Truth be told, some of the most arrogant people on this silly planet are those who stubbornly insist on regarding themselves as worthless and insignificant despite God having quite clearly told them the exact opposite.

Misconception #2: Humble = Weak

Neither does "humble" mean "weak" or "mamby-pamby."

Jesus described Himself as "humble" (Matthew 11:29) yet His many "up-in-their-business" confrontations with the Pharisees as well as His driving out the money-changers from the Temple with a whip could hardly be characterized as wimpy. That doesn't even begin to touch on the fact He carried His cross to Golgotha after enduring horrific torture none of us could imagine experiencing, much less enduring.

Neither were His disciples Caspar Milquetoasts once they had received the New Birth (John 20:21) and been baptized in the Holy Spirit at Pentecost. Wimps don't endure life-threatening hardships including floggings, stonings, death, imprisonment, and shipwreck, or boldly speak truth to power on multiple occasions.

All but the Apostle John were martyred for their faith. They tried to include John in that list by boiling him in oil, but the man supernaturally couldn't be cooked. In their desperation to get him out of both their hair and the public eye, Rome exiled him to the Isle of Patmos where he later wrote the Book of Revelation between shifts working in a mine.

Weak? Mamby-pamby? Wimpy? *I don't think so!*

Which leaves us asking the musical question: *what is humility and how do we get it?*

My Own Journey Towards Humility

Setting the Stage

My journey began unbeknownst-to-me-at-the-time in the mid-1990s when I first encountered a book entitled *The Final Quest* by Rick Joyner.

This one book has by far had the most significant impact upon my walk with God outside the Bible. This chapter substantiates that claim, so read on!

At that point in my life, I lived in Tulsa, Oklahoma. I was a lazy, arrogant, self-absorbed, self-directed, pornography-addicted, narcissistic rageaholic. My badly troubled marriage was a hollow shell held together only by "thou shalt not divorce."

While my late-ex certainly had her own set of issues back then, the primary source for the vast majority of our relational problems was that bozo staring back at me in the mirror each morning. As a husband and father, I was absolutely no treat to live with.

Several of the marriage counselors we engaged in our futile attempts to make things better placed most of the blame squarely where it belonged: *me!* One counselor got so exasperated, he actually took me aside out of my wife's presence and rebuked me with the literal words, *"Stop being such an a--hole!"*

Need I say more?

So when I first encountered that book, I was a *mess*. My prayer life was virtually nonexistent. My walk with God was a shadow of what it could or should have been. I had a near-encyclopedic head-knowledge of much of God's Word, but had zero fruit to show for it.

Bottom line? I was a worthless asset in God's plan to further His Kingdom.

Enter *The Final Quest*

A customer of our graphic design business recommended this book, describing it as "compelling" and "transformative." Since she was a book editor for a Christian publisher as well as a friend, her opinion carried some weight with us — this was high praise indeed!

So we bought a copy and read it.

Two concepts reached out and grabbed me by the heart in that initial reading:

1. The standards God uses to judge value and success are completely alien to the utterly corrupt ones we use as human beings — even as Christ-followers.
2. The author had prayed for God to judge him strictly in this life so he would not receive harsh judgments in the next.

Somehow or another, I managed to pray something along the lines of #2 in the list.

And so it began…

All God had been waiting for was my permission for Him to start messing with my business. Once He had it, He almost immediately started answering that prayer by popping my bubble of complacency.

First on His agenda? My sex addiction.

Here's how that played out. One weekday morning as I woke up typically late, I was stunned to discover my wife had left me.

No histrionics, no ultimatums, no goodbye, not even a note; zip, zilch, nada, gone. She and the minivan had simply disappeared into thin air!

In time, she rented her own house, bought her own car, and, as things with me steadily worsened as I floundered about trying to cope with the major paradigm shift of my new reality, both our son and foster-son eventually moved out to be with her instead.

For awhile, we continued to operate our home-based business together, albeit in separate households. Leading up to her departure, my side of our business operations had been steadily drying up and I was simply too lazy to do much to remedy the problem — she ended up carrying the entire financial load.

As my share of the income-stream dwindled, I started working occasional short-term jobs through a temp agency. I eventually began seriously hunting for a permanent position while collecting unemployment benefits. To meet my weekly quota of applications, I sent out my resume in response to any IT- or graphics-related newspaper ad (remember those?) I came across whether I truly wanted the position or not — or was even remotely qualified for it.

The Move to Wichita

Not long after my wife left me, a tech company in Wichita, Kansas called me to set up an interview. It turned out to be one of those "throw-away" applications I had submitted merely to maintain my unemployment payments. Amazingly, they made me a nice enough offer including relocation assistance that I accepted it.

So I packed up my stuff and moved 3 hours northwest into a nice townhouse. My new digs were large enough to house the family in anticipation of our son's visits and, as it later turned out, reunification with my wife. Once I was there, she relinquished her rental home and moved back into our house in Broken Arrow, immediately putting it on the market.

By the providence of God, I was exactly where He wanted me!

Addiction Recovery

Once settled in Wichita, I started attending a church which operates a counseling center. Dr. Troy Reiner, its founder and director, is by far the most gifted and anointed Christian counsellor I've ever encountered.

Christ-centered support groups meet every Wednesday night in lieu of a mid-week service. Alcoholism, drug-abuse, codependency, anger management, sex/pornography addiction, abuse recovery, weight-loss, you name it, they have a meeting for it! Groups meet in every room of the church, including the pastor's office. Because the State of Kansas' legal system recognizes the validity of faith-based counseling solutions, people can receive their court-ordered treatment there.

It's awesome!

Sooooo… I joined the sexual addiction group. Over time, I received two major revelations:

3. While I was truly a mess, I wasn't half as screwed up as the rest of the guys present. I found hope in that despite the fact I had been addicted from childhood.

4. I already possessed many of the keys required for my recovery: the Word of Faith teachings I received for over a decade. I had simply never thought to use them to open this particular prison door.

So I did the work needed to recover. Things got better. My wife eventually sold the house in Tulsa and moved to Wichita. We began couples therapy with Dr. Reiner immediately upon her arrival. After a time, she moved back in with me. Our marriage improved drastically (though not to where it was invulnerable to the fatal attack lurking a few years down the road).

I loved our time in Wichita. It remains my all-time favorite city to live in for reasons way too numerous to recount here. If the Lord ever gave us the go-ahead to return there, I'd gladly move back in a New York minute!

In retrospect, it felt like I was basking in God's favor as my life moved onto a far firmer footing.

Good times!

Our Move to Tampa

In 1998, I was laid off from my second job in Wichita, one I truly loved: webmaster for an industry-leading electronics manufacturer.

When my close friend, the founder/president of Life Christian University, heard I was available, he invited us to move to the Tampa Bay Area of Florida so I could work for him. We took a trip down there to spy out the land and felt like God was in it, so we moved to Florida where I became LCU's Director of Communications & Information Technology.

Things went extremely well for several years.

Professionally, I redesigned their course catalog and student handbook, degree certificates, and official transcripts; built their first website; designed all their forms (establishing a form design pattern still in use, I might add); converted the university's computing environment from Windows to macOS (they remain an all-Mac shop to this day); and wrote the first version of Cyber-Registrar™, the database application they use to manage their student records. 24 years and 3 versions later, that software is still in use, all those versions written by yours truly.

Ministry-wise, I also earned my Associates and Bachelors degrees and began work on a Masters in Christian Counseling. I was licensed as a minister and later ordained. I launched a Bible-based support group which was bearing significant fruit in the lives of our participants and my work there had earned the respect of my counseling professor. I was also being used in the charismatic gifts in our church's services.

Am I proud of all those accomplishments? Obviously.

Could I have pulled any of it off apart from the Lord?

Not a snowball's chance in… well, *that* place!

Bottom line? Life was *good!*

The Other Shoe Drops

All that being said, God still needed to address 3 remaining near-fatal spiritual and character flaws in me:

1. My adulterous heart

Though clean and sober regarding things sexual, I constantly fantasized about being married to other women I encountered, something I had struggled with my entire life. Largely due to this, our marriage remained fatally rotten at its core, thus leaving me vulnerable to Satan's next major attack in 2001.

2. My prayerlessness

I knew intellectually what the Scriptures say about prayer, faith, and other related topics, but little of it was in my heart. That head-knowledge quickly became extremely practical when my net worth was whatever I could find in my wallet at any given moment.

3. My colossal ego

My head was so big, it would have fit in proportionally with the faces on Mt. Rushmore. I was completely convinced I was God's Great Gift to the ministry in general and Christian counseling specifically, absolutely confident I had all my ducks in a row, head-to-tail, and evenly spaced.

(For those of you who may have been lulled to sleep during my interminable storytelling, our current topic is humility. Remember humility? This is a chapter about humility.)

Humility Through Humiliation

Those 3 words summarize the following 7 years or so as God allowed me to repeatedly crash my arrogance upon the Chief Cornerstone of His Son until it eventually broke and I humbled myself at His feet once and for all.

I just ran across a verse in the OT today describing that process. In 2 Chronicles, it recounts the conquering of Jerusalem by the Egyptian king Shishak and describes why God permitted that defeat as well as how He was going to use it:

> *...Since the people have humbled themselves, I will not completely destroy them and will soon give them some relief. I will not use Shishak to pour out My anger on Jerusalem.* ***But they will become his subjects, so they will know the difference between serving me and serving earthly rulers.***
>
> *2 Chronicles 12:7b–8 NLT (emphasis mine)*

Bottom line? Serving an earthly ruler (myself) sucks!

Once that issue was settled between us, things calmed down and God was able to start blessing me again. I met and married my wife (a continual source of further lessons in humility to this day!). I went back to work for LCU after a 7-year hiatus and remained there for just over 15 years. My relationship with my son was eventually restored. I started writing my blog and later became a published author. I finished my masters degree and went on to earn 2 doctorates.

God restored all those years the locusts of my arrogant self-lordship had eaten — and well beyond that!

Life again is *good!*

What Does the Word Say?

The Bible verses on this topic could fill a book. Truth be told, they already do fill quite a few books, most of them found in the OT. Arrogance is closely associated with idolatry and even a cursory study of the Scriptures clearly demonstrates:

- The tight conceptual linkage between the two in the mind of our Creator;
- His displeasure with either/both of them, as well as;
- The tragic consequences experienced by those who stubbornly "went there".

I will be discussing in Chapter 6 how our spiritual authority over the powers of darkness is directly dependent upon our humble submission to the Most High. I've also addressed how our ability to cast our earthly cares upon the Lord is equally contingent upon such an attitude.

In both places, I cited the following verses where James and Peter identically paraphrase Proverbs 3:34:

> *God opposes the proud but gives grace to the humble.*
>
> *James 4:61; Peter 5:5*

The key words in those verses are both evocative and compelling in the Greek:

proud (*huperephanos*)

> *showing one's self above others, overtopping, conspicuous above others, pre-eminent; having an presumptuous estimate of one's means or merits, despising others or even treating them with contempt, haughty, cavalier*

resist (*antitassomai*)

to range in battle against; to oppose one's self; to resist

In other words, the all-powerful Creator of everything we see Who perfectly knows the hearts and minds of all of us — takes notice of our arrogant attitudes (no matter how thoroughly we have deluded ourselves) *-and-* then sets Himself in battle array against us in each and every case until we give up.

Gee, I wonder who's going to win that match-up? *Oops!*

Here is an aphorism I coined years ago:

> *Lordship is proven only when there is a difference of opinion between you and God — and He wins!*

There is no sliding scale here: deliberate disobedience in 2% of your life is 100% rebellion in God's eyes.

If you've got a problem with my conclusions, I didn't make any of it up. He said it.

- Clearly
- Directly
- Repeatedly
- Consistently
- Out loud
- Without equivocation
- To many people
- Throughout history
- Without one single exception

After careful, exhaustive examination of the Scriptures, I can assure you with absolute certainty that God has *never* lost a battle *without exception*. He is infinitely stronger, infinitely smarter, and infinitely more patient than any of us could ever hope to be.

The Solution

The solution is ridiculously simple to describe, yet requires the grace of God to pull off: *repentance.*

The following Greek word is translated "repent" throughout the NT:

repent (*metanoeo*)

> *to change one's mind for better, heartily to amend with abhorrence of one's past sins*
>
> *So repent **[change your inner self—your old way of thinking, regret past sins] and return [to God—seek His purpose for your life]**, so that your sins may be wiped away [blotted out, completely erased], **so that times of refreshing may come from the presence of the Lord** [restoring you like a cool wind on a hot day];*
>
> *Acts 3:19 AMP (emphasis mine)*

Repentance is both an event and a journey. In other words, our initial repentance event occurs when we surrender to Jesus as Lord. However, that is merely the beginning of our journey of repentance. We walk out that odyssey by deliberately and repeatedly choosing to do things His way instead of our own.

That activity progressively infuses His ways of assessing and doing things into our very beings, replacing what otherwise comes to us naturally. The $10 theological term for this process is "sanctification."

A Lifestyle of Repentance

We engage in this exercise by:

- Surrendering to Him as living sacrifices (Romans 12:1)
- Not allowing ourselves to be pressured into conforming to pop culture narratives (Romans 12:2a) or religious expectations arising from our doctrinal heritage/alignment, for that matter.
- Being transformed by His Word and Spirit into thinking, acting, and reacting like He does in our relationships (Romans 12:2b)
- Boldly coming before God's throne of grace to seek mercy, grace, and help when it all either appears impossible to pull off — or we have miserably failed (Hebrews 4:16)

In other words, repentance is nowhere close to the dead religious works defined by man's religion:

- Do this, don't do that
- Cut this off, grow that out
- Don't touch, don't taste
- Beat our breasts
- Flagellate ourselves
- Light candles
- Crawl across broken glass
- Make pilgrimages
- Do penance
- *Mea culpa, mea culpa, mea maxima culpa, ad infinitum, ad nauseam.*

Instead, repentance is a life-style of humility before the Most High, letting His standards of thinking and behavior replace our fleshly ones.

Yes, repentance requires us to walk away from our pet sins and ask His forgiveness. But once that's done, we're to leave that junk — along its attendant guilt and shame — in our rearview mirrors and place our laser focus on Jesus, "the Author and Perfecter of our faith."

Therein lies joy and freedom!

The Practice of Daily Surrender

One of the ways I fuel my personal movement towards humility is by re-centering my focus on reality. How? Through a daily affirmation/ confession of surrender. So my morning prayers begin with something along the lines of:

> *Lord, I humble myself before You and surrender to You because You are Lord and I'm not. I roll the cares of today over onto You because You care for me. All my needs are met through Your riches in glory by Christ Jesus.*
>
> *Satan, you may not steal, kill, and destroy in my life today in the name of Jesus! Shut up and get out!*

What have I just accomplished in the spirit realm? By faith, I have:

1. Recentered in my consciousness this is God's day — *not mine!* — to run.

2. Positioned myself to receive God's promises.

3. Asserted the day's pecking order: God, then me, then the powers of darkness who must cease and desist their attacks upon me.

That practice has been working swimmingly over a decade and counting. My last words on this planet will be probably be something along those same lines.

In Conclusion

Humility?

- It's humanity's only acceptable response to God.
- It's vital to our walk with Jesus.
- It's inescapably at the forefront of all His dealings with us.

CHAPTER

4

Humility: Part 2

IN THIS CHAPTER, WE'RE GOING TO CONTINUE exploring the topic of humility, this time from a different angle. As I was reading in 2 Chronicles the other day, I came across a passage well-known in Word of Faith (WoF) circles, one I have lost count of the times I've heard taught in sermons:

> *After this, the armies of the Moabites, Ammonites, and some of the Meunites declared war on Jehoshaphat. Messengers came and told Jehoshaphat, "A vast army from Edom is marching against you from beyond the Dead Sea. They are already at Hazazon-tamar." (This was another name for En-gedi.)*
>
> *Jehoshaphat was terrified by this news and begged the Lord for guidance. He also ordered everyone in Judah to begin fasting. So people from all the towns of Judah came to Jerusalem to seek the Lord's help.*
>
> *Jehoshaphat stood before the community of Judah and Jerusalem in front of the new courtyard at the Temple of the Lord. He prayed,*

"O Lord, God of our ancestors, You alone are the God Who is in heaven. You are ruler of all the kingdoms of the earth. You are powerful and mighty; no one can stand against You!

"O our God, did You not drive out those who lived in this land when Your people Israel arrived? And did you not give this land forever to the descendants of Your friend Abraham? Your people settled here and built this Temple to honor Your name. They said, 'Whenever we are faced with any calamity such as war, plague, or famine, we can come to stand in Your presence before this Temple where Your name is honored. We can cry out to You to save us, and You will hear us and rescue us.'

"And now see what the armies of Ammon, Moab, and Mount Seir are doing. You would not let our ancestors invade those nations when Israel left Egypt, so they went around them and did not destroy them. Now see how they reward us! For they have come to throw us out of Your land, which You gave us as an inheritance. O our God, won't You stop them? We are powerless against this mighty army that is about to attack us. We do not know what to do, but we are looking to You for help."

As all the men of Judah stood before the Lord with their little ones, wives, and children, the Spirit of the Lord came upon one of the men standing there. His name was Jahaziel, son of Zechariah, son of Benaiah, son of Jeiel, son of Mattaniah, a Levite who was a descendant of Asaph.

He said, "Listen, all you people of Judah and Jerusalem! Listen, King Jehoshaphat! This is what the Lord says: 'Do not be afraid! Don't be discouraged by this mighty army, for the battle is not yours, but God's. Tomorrow, march out against them. You will find them coming up through the Ascent of Ziz at the end of the valley that opens into the wilderness of Jeruel. But you will not even need to fight. Take your positions; then stand still and watch the Lord's victory. He is with you, O people of Judah and Jerusalem. Do not be afraid or discouraged. Go out against them tomorrow, for the Lord is with you!'"

Then King Jehoshaphat bowed low with his face to the ground. And all the people of Judah and Jerusalem did the same, worshiping the Lord. Then the Levites from the clans of Kohath and Korah stood to praise the Lord, the God of Israel, with a very loud shout.

Early the next morning the army of Judah went out into the wilderness of Tekoa. On the way Jehoshaphat stopped and said, "Listen to me, all you people of Judah and Jerusalem! Believe in the Lord your God, and you will be able to stand firm. Believe in his prophets, and you will succeed."

After consulting the people, the king appointed singers to walk ahead of the army, singing to the Lord and praising him for his holy splendor. This is what they sang:

"Give thanks to the Lord; his faithful love endures forever!"

At the very moment they began to sing and give praise, the Lord caused the armies of Ammon, Moab, and Mount Seir to start fighting among themselves. The armies of Moab and Ammon turned against their allies from Mount Seir and killed every one of them. After they had destroyed the army of Seir, they began attacking each other. So when the army of Judah arrived at the lookout point in the wilderness, all they saw were dead bodies lying on the ground as far as they could see. Not a single one of the enemy had escaped.

King Jehoshaphat and his men went out to gather the plunder. They found vast amounts of equipment, clothing, and other valuables — more than they could carry. There was so much plunder that it took them three days just to collect it all! On the

> *fourth day they gathered in the Valley of Blessing, which got its name that day because the people praised and thanked the Lord there. It is still called the Valley of Blessing today.*
>
> *Then all the men returned to Jerusalem, with Jehoshaphat leading them, overjoyed that the Lord had given them victory over their enemies. They marched into Jerusalem to the music of harps, lyres, and trumpets, and they proceeded to the Temple of the Lord.*
>
> *2 Chronicles 20:1–28 NLT*

Every WoF sermon I've ever heard on this story focusses on the topics of faith and worship. This is entirely valid and I am neither negating nor taking away anything from what I've heard taught along those lines from this passage. We're simply going to examine this account from a slightly different perspective.

Jehoshaphat Surrendered

No, not to the army arrayed against Judah, but to God Almighty. Rather than complaining about the overwhelmingly terrible situation, he humbled himself before God despite his being scared out of his wits. He not only sought His wisdom personally, he led Judah into the same quality of surrender by commanding a nationwide fast.

Amazingly, we see no hint of resistance on their part, only the entire nation joining their king in submission to the Most High. While statistically, there certainly would have been a few holdouts to Jehoshaphat's plan, any such minority was so insignificant the historian recounting the story didn't feel the need to mention them. Neither did their possible presence effect the final outcome.

Can you imagine the American church-at-large responding with similar humility and obedience to such a demand made by our president (assuming we ever had a president of like humility to Jehoshaphat)? Yeah, right — *That* could happen!

I can imagine the clamors of protest with folks saying things like,

- Who does he think he is, demanding us to stop eating. He's violating the separation of church and state!", or;
- "Isn't there alternative which doesn't require this kind of sacrifice? I have children to think of!" or;
- "I think we should negotiate with our enemies. Once they see how nice we are, they'll leave us alone!" or;
- "Why is God doing this to us? It simply isn't fair!"

But I digress...

First, evil can never be negotiated with, mollified, or appeased, only opposed and destroyed. Neville Chamberlain and Great Britain learned that to their great sorrow dealing with Hitler. Hundreds of thousands, possibly millions, died because of Chamberlain's spinelessness and wishful thinking. Had he remained in power, rather than being replaced by Churchill, it is entirely likely the British would be speaking German today. Oops! Digressing again!

So how *do* we oppose evil? *With overwhelming force!*

And where do we get overwhelming force when we don't have any on hand?

From Overwhelming-Force-R-Us, the almighty Lord of Hosts!

How do we get Him to fight on our behalf? *Surrender to Him!*

And that is precisely what Jehoshaphat and Judah did.

Jehoshaphat Obeyed

When Jahaziel, the man God chose to speak through, proclaimed the Word of the Lord, Jehoshaphat didn't question, he didn't second-guess. He humbly worshipped and simply obeyed.

Many believers in the WoF specifically and the Body of Christ in general enthusiastically embrace the worship portion of that equation, but minimize or outright ignore God's requirement for ongoing humility and even more crucially: *exacting obedience.*

Furthermore, Jehoshaphat didn't add to or subtract from what he was told. Unlike the tendency of typical modern-day Christians, he didn't take God's command as a launchpad for impromptu personal creativity, riffing a divinely-inspired-but-human-reason-polluted plan of action like a soloist's improvisation on a musical theme during a jazz performance.

Why is this crucial?

Given the fact God is truly infinite and all-knowing, it is logical to conclude He has knowledge, insights, and wisdom inconceivable to our limited-by-space-and-time and corrupted-by-sinful-flesh perceptions of reality. Again, as I once said in a blog article on double-mindedness (there's a link to it in this book's appendix), many real, but avoidable, problems begin when we think or do the equivalent of, "Here, God, hold my beer; I've got this!"

The Boy & The Snake

I'm reminded of a story I once heard about an American pastor on a missionary journey to Central Africa. As he was standing outside the church talking to the local pastor, the pastor's young son was playing under a nearby tree.

Suddenly, the pastor shouted out, *"Son! Drop to the ground!"*

The boy immediately obeyed.

The pastor continued, this time shouting, *"Now crawl towards me as fast as you can!"*

Once again the boy instantly complied.

A few moments later, the pastor again shouted to his son, *"Now stand up and run to me!"*

Again, instant obedience.

When the boy reached his side, the pastor pointed back at the tree. Moments later, all three of them saw a huge black mamba — the most aggressive and deadliest venomous snake species in Africa — drop out of that tree onto the very spot where the boy had been playing.

Had the boy not explicitly trusted his father and unquestioningly obeyed him without hesitation, he would never have survived the snake-bite; mamba venom is so incredibly toxic he would have died long before they could have driven off the snake and then obtained medical treatment. A typical American child would have whined, argued, and resisted, thereby becoming the honoree at his own funeral.

God's commands are frequently no less life-and-death kinds of instructions. We often ignore them to our peril. When the terrorist attacks occurred on 9/11, quite a few Christ-followers were supposed to be at work in the World Trade Center that day, but were told by the Lord, directly or indirectly, to not go in to work. The ones who obeyed watched in horror from the safety of their own homes as those who didn't listen died in the collapses of their shared workplace.

Selah!

The Laptop

Sometimes we never see any results of our obedience or even know the reason why. Case-in-point: a renowned WoF minister and author named Rick Renner related the following story to us during a sermon.

He was one of the keynote speakers at a WoF convention. He was getting dressed to attend one of the evening meetings where he was not scheduled to speak, but was expected to make an appearance nonetheless. The Holy Spirit had other ideas, though; He clearly and distinctly told Rick to stay right there in his hotel room. He argued with the Lord about how everyone was expecting him to be at the meeting.

The Holy Spirit persisted. Rick resisted.

Finally, there was a knock at his hotel room door. Thinking it was his driver there to pick him up for the meeting, Rick shouted out, "I'm almost ready to leave! I'll be out in a few minutes!" About 10 minutes later, he disobediently left his room, took the elevator downstairs, got into the car, and departed for the meeting, all while the Holy Spirit continued telling him to go back.

When Rick returned to his hotel after the meeting had ended several hours later, he discovered his room had been burgled and his laptop computer stolen. He later realized the knock on his door had been the burglar checking to see if the room was occupied, not Rick's driver. The real tragedy of that theft was Rick's laptop had the almost-completed manuscript for his newest book on its hard drive and there was no backup anywhere!

Hours and hours of labor had simply evaporated into thin air with no other remedy than to start over from scratch and rewrite the book. (I'll also guarantee you Rick immediately reevaluated his abysmal backup strategy!)

We are then left to ponder the musical question: what would have happened had Rick obeyed?

In a word: *nothing!*

Not. One. Blessed. Thing.

The thief would have discovered the room was occupied and then moved on to easier pickings. This would have left Rick scratching his head, wondering if he had actually heard from God or not. But his laptop and book manuscript would have remained safely in his possession.

God's Attitude Towards Disobedience

God's high priority on obedience can be summed up nicely with His response to King Saul's disobedience as recorded in 1 Samuel 15.

Setting the Stage

- God told Saul to attack and utterly destroy the city-state of Amalek, killing every man, woman, child, and animal there by the edge of the sword.
- The Amalekites had constantly harassed the Israelites during the Exodus. Their favorite practice was to ambush the tail-end of the convoy and either kill or enslave the stragglers. If pregnant women were among the stragglers, their unborn children were cut from their wombs with a sword and both were left to die on the sand. By that point in history, the Amalekites had exhausted God's grace and mercy and He had had His fill of these bozos.

  What skeptics who accuse God of genocide — and even more tragically, many Christians — don't realize is the Amalekites, as well as all the other nearby pagan nations, were given over to sexual immorality as part of their idol worship. As a result, every man and woman was infected with one or more venereal diseases. Because incest and bestiality were two of their many sexual perversions, even their children and livestock were infected.

Please note this took place during the Bronze Age when germ theory and antibiotics were several millennia in the future. The only way these then-incurable diseases could be prevented from infecting the Israelites was by the total annihilation of all infected pagans as well as their animals.

- Saul partially obeyed by attacking and destroying the city.
- But he kept alive Agag, the king of Amalek.
- Saul also had his army sort out the critters and only destroy those which seemed worthless or undesirable while preserving whatever seemed good and desirable in their own eyes.
- God sent Samuel to rebuke Saul.
- Saul lied to Samuel, claiming he had obeyed.
- Samuel called out Saul for his disobedience and dishonesty.
- Saul tried to deflect, claiming he kept the animals alive to sacrifice to God (unbeknownst to him, they were unacceptable to God as sacrifices because they were diseased).
- Samuel called Saul out again, this time adding arrogance to the charges.
- Saul finally owned his disobedience for keeping Agag alive, but immediately tried to shift the blame to his army for the livestock, reiterating the animals were kept alive for sacrifice to the Lord.

The Tragic Ending

Samuel then pronounces God's judgment on Saul, the beginning of the end for both him and his dynasty:

> *What is more pleasing to the Lord: your burnt offerings and sacrifices or your obedience to His voice?*
>
> *Listen! Obedience is better than sacrifice, and submission is better than offering the fat of rams. Rebellion is as sinful as witchcraft, and stubbornness as bad as worshiping idols.*
>
> *So because you have rejected the command of the Lord, He has rejected you as king. — 1 Samuel 15:22-23 NLT*

Since that passage is clearly and unequivocally stated, I feel like I have nothing to add here.

In Conclusion

Our complete inability to obey our Creator apart from His limitless grace and the indwelling power of the Holy Spirit is the very reason God-in-Sandals had to show up in the first place. In other words, if we could do any of this on our own spin, then Jesus died needlessly.

As I have already stated, I have absolutely not "arrived" in that endeavor and will never perfectly achieve perfection this side of eternity.

Same goes for you, too!

Which leads us back to those verses in James and 1 Peter I cited in the previous chapter:

> *...God gives grace to the humble.*

Our path of obedience is paved with His grace. We receive His grace through our humility.

To paraphrase James 2:20: *"Faith without obedience is dead."*

- There are no alternatives.

- Workarounds are nonexistent.
- Detours are not permitted.
- Do-overs are rarely, if ever, granted.

It's all right there in front of us written in black and white (sometimes red and white):

OBEY!

And then witness our amazing, all-powerful, all-loving, all-knowing God move mightily on our behalf.

> *For the eyes of the Lord run to and fro throughout the whole earth, to show Himself strong on behalf of those whose heart is loyal to Him… — 2 Chronicles 16:9aå*

CHAPTER

5

Our Covenant With God

THE TERM "COVENANT" IS CASUALLY TOSSED about in many churches by sincere, well-meaning pastors and laypersons alike with many of them having only a nebulous grasp of what a covenant truly is, what one entails, and why this specific biblical term defines a Christ-follower's relationship with the Most High God.

Our familiarity with that word mostly comes from our hearing it every time we drink the grape juice or wine during communion:

> *This is the blood of the new covenant, which is poured out for many for the forgiveness of sins. — Matthew 26:28*

Both Mark and Luke echo almost identical phrasing in their accounts.

So What's a Covenant?

The concept of a blood covenant ("blood covenant" is actually a far more accurate term than the term "covenant" used by itself) is both incredibly ancient and 100% biblical. The Old Testament recounts several examples of people entering into blood covenant relationships with one another. The covenant between then-soon-to-be-king David and King Saul's son Jonathan is one which immediately comes to mind. A modern-day counterpart is the concept of "blood brothers" as celebrated in classic movies and TV series about the Wild West.

The Abrahamic Covenant

One of the most important covenant relationships in human history was the one between God and Abraham.

Why?

This covenant laid the foundation for our redemption in the finished work of Jesus Christ centuries later.

The details of how people established covenants are not pertinent to our discussion here, whereas the results and benefits of being in one is crucial. When two people entered a blood covenant with one another, each was pledging with his own blood that all their own property, family, and wealth were at the complete disposal of the other party and to each party's descendants in perpetuity. We see this concept echoed in the marriage covenant to this day: all the earthly goods of the husband and wife become mutual (community) property — at least in most states and in the absence of a pre-nup, that is!

So when God entered into covenant with Abraham, He was saying to Abraham, "Everything I have is yours extending to your descendants in perpetuity," and Abraham was saying to God, "Everything I have and that my descendants will ever have — including our very lives — is Yours in perpetuity."

This is what theologians call the "Abrahamic Covenant."

Abraham & Isaac at Mt. Moriah

We now approach an account in Genesis where many people — quite a few of them theologians, I might add — simply cannot seem to get it right: the story of God commanding Abraham to sacrifice his son Isaac to Him. I have heard more cockamamie, half-baked nonsense about this single story than just about any other story in the entire Bible — other than the entire book of Job, that is!

To establish context, we find the account of God starting His relationship with Abraham (then Abram) in Genesis 12, His establishment of a covenant with Abraham in chapter 17, and this specific story in chapter 22. The intervening chapters are informative, but not directly applicable to this discussion.

Please note in this story how Abraham didn't quibble with God about the issue — he simply packed up his son and their accoutrements and headed off for Mount Moriah.

Why?

Because he knew the requirements of a covenant.

We all know what happened there: as Abraham's knife was descending to kill his son, the Lord stayed his hand and told him his willingness alone proved his faith in and obedience to the Lord. Hebrews 11:17-19 states Abraham so believed God's promise he fully expected God to raise Isaac from the dead once he had obeyed — all this with zero historical precedent, I might add!

In this way, Abraham showed he was willing to sacrifice his beloved son for his covenant partner, God. This event, standing alone, has no historical significance and therefore means almost nothing, thus explaining why so many scholars — especially Jewish ones — come up with such ridiculous interpretations for it.

God Closes the Loop

The historical context and true significance of that event on Mt. Moriah surfaces about 2 millennia later when God repaid Abraham's willingness in kind by actually sacrificing His only Son, Jesus Christ, on the cross — interestingly enough, in the selfsame location, give or take a few yards — and purchase the redemption of Abraham's descendants (the Jews) as well as all mankind who would accept His gift by faith.

That is why Christianity honors Abraham as the "father of our faith."

The Mosaic Covenant

A subsequent covenant based in the Law of Moses, known as the Mosaic Covenant, was introduced a little over 400 years after Abraham. That covenant ended with the death, burial, and resurrection of Jesus and the implementation of the New Covenant in Jesus' blood.

The New Covenant in Jesus' Blood

As we've already mentioned, the New Covenant in Jesus' blood is precisely that: new! The Greek word for "new" in these passages is *kainos*:

new (*kainos*)

of a new kind, unprecedented, novel, uncommon, unheard of

This means those of us submitting to Jesus' lordship over our lives are operating in a uniquely distinctive relationship with The One True God, a covenant relationship with no precedent and having never existed prior to Jesus' sacrifice on the cross.

So the Mosaic Covenant has been superceded by a new and better one. Why is it better? The New Testament clearly states its superiority comes from it being based on better promises (Hebrews 8:6) the foremost among them being grace!

The implications of our covenant with God are the selfsame as Abraham's: everything we have is God's and everything God has is ours!

Though the Mosaic Covenant has been superseded by the New Covenant in Jesus' blood, the Abrahamic Covenant has never been rescinded, dissolved, or otherwise nullified. Indeed, Paul states in Galatians 3 that the New Covenant is actually an extension of the Abrahamic Covenant, giving us believers the benefits of both.

> *I will make you a great nation; I will bless you and make your name great; and you shall be a blessing. I will bless those who bless you, and I will curse him who curses you; and in you all the families of the earth shall be blessed. — Genesis 12:2-3*

> *Christ has redeemed us from the curse of the law, having become a curse for us (for it is written, "Cursed is everyone who hangs on a tree"), 14 that the blessing of Abraham might come upon the Gentiles in Christ Jesus, that we might receive the promise of the Spirit through faith... And if you are Christ's, then you are Abraham's seed, and heirs according to the promise.*
> *— Galatians 3:13-14,29*

We Christians are now a great nation, a spiritual one headed by the King of Kings and Lord of Lords. We are a blessing to the earth and all its families.

God will bless them that bless us and curse them that curse us.

The bottom line is this: when we entered into salvation, we gave everything we have and are to God, and in return, He has given us everything He has and everything He is.

Wow! We definitely got the better end of that deal!

When you make this fundamental concept of Christian theology foundational to your walk with Christ, it completely redefines our approach prayer, giving us the courage to "come boldly to the throne of grace, that we may obtain mercy and find grace to help in time of need."

CHAPTER

6

Our Authority as Believers

ANOTHER FOUNDATIONAL CONCEPT FOR AN effective prayer life is our authority in Christ. To be certain, you can enjoy a modicum of success without internalizing this salient theological fact, but you will essentially fight with one spiritual hand tied behind your back.

Before I continue, let me be perfectly clear: *God is indeed sovereign.* He is the Supreme Ruler of the Universe. On top of that, He has invested 100% of His authority in Jesus as King of Kings and Lord of Lords:

> *Christ himself was like God in everything. But he did not think that being equal with God was something to be used for his own benefit. But he gave up his place with God and made himself nothing. He was born as a man and became like a servant. And when he was living as a man, he humbled himself and was fully obedient to God,even when that caused his death — death on a cross.*

> *So God raised him to the highest place. God made his name greater than every other name so that every knee will bow to the name of Jesus — everyone in heaven, on earth, and under the earth. And everyone will confess that Jesus Christ is Lord and bring glory to God the Father. — Philippians 2:6-11 NCV*

What most people do is take this sovereignty concept to extremes, using it as the be-all, end-all answer to all questions. We can sum their conceptual foundation up as follows:

> *God is sovereign and totally in charge. Therefore, everything which happens on earth is by His will, whether by direct causation or permissive inaction.*

First, this is faulty reasoning, absurdity at its worst. If this statement were indeed true, we must also conclude those who are unsaved are not so because it's God's will for them to be that way (Calvinism's predestination nonsense). Another implication is that when other people sin against us, they are doing so at the impetus — or with the permission — of the Almighty. That idea would also logically imply we ourselves are personally not responsible for our sins.

"But wait!" you say. "The Bible clearly says that it's God's will for everyone to be saved!"

Good answer!

So our logical conclusion must be there are indeed events and human choices taking place on this earth which are not God's will. Think about it for a minute: *why would Jesus have commanded us in the Lord's Prayer to pray for God's will to be done on earth as it is in heaven if His will is already being done here?*

The second problem with the aforementioned Calvinist/Catholic (which is actually Augustinian) philosophical foundation concerning God's sovereignty is the last half of the first sentence in that statement is absolutely incorrect. Why? Because there are other authorities involved!

"But hold it there, Steve!" you might exclaim. "You just said that God is sovereign!"

He is, *period.*

However, He has also delegated much of His authority on this earth to others and they, in turn, have surrendered it to yet others.

God Gave Man Dominion Over the Earth

The Book of Genesis establishes this concept succinctly:

> *'So God created man in His image; in the image of God He created him; male and female He created them. Then God blessed them, and God said to them, "Be fruitful and multiply; fill the earth and* ***subdue it; have dominion*** *over the fish of the sea, over the birds of the air, and over every living thing that moves on the earth.' — Genesis 2:27-29 (emphasis mine)*

The words "subdue" and "have dominion" come from the following Hebrew words:

subdue(*kawbash*)

> *to subdue, to make subservient, to bring into bondage, to dominate*

have dominion(*radah*)

> *to have dominion, to rule, to subjugate*

From this passage, we see how God delegated His own authority over the earth to mankind. That means man had control — under God — over the earth and all it contained.

Man Handed Dominion Over to Satan

So what did Adam do with the authority delegated to him by God? He surrendered it by submitting to a false god — Satan — in Chapter 3.

How do we know this transfer took place? Because the New Testament states it repeatedly. John 12:31; 14:30; 16:11 all quote Jesus Himself as calling him "the ruler of this world."

Here are the Greek words for "ruler" and "world:"

ruler (*archon*)

> *ruler, commander, chief, leader*

world (*cosmos*)

> *the world, the universe; the circle of the earth, the earth; the inhabitants of the earth, men, the human family, the ungodly multitude; the whole mass of men alienated from God, and therefore hostile to the cause of Christ; world affairs, the aggregate of things earthly;*
>
> *the whole circle of earthly goods, endowments, riches, advantages, pleasures, etc, which although hollow and frail and fleeting, stir desire, seduce from God and are obstacles to the cause of Christ*

Paul in Ephesians 2:2 calls Satan the "prince of the power of the air." Here again we see the word *archon* again, this time translated as the word "prince." The word "power" is the Greek word *exousia* and "air" is the Greek word *ær*."

power (*exousia*)

> *the power of him whose will and commands must be submitted to by others and obeyed*

air (*ær*)

> *the atmospheric region*

The title literally means *"the ruler with complete authority over the atmospheric region."*

The Legal Rationale for Prayer

Why else do you think God works through men on this earth? If He had not bound Himself by His Word to that original delegation of authority back in Eden, He could have simply acted unilaterally — He certainly has the power and the desire to wipe out evil on this earth, hasn't He? His omnipotence means He certainly doesn't need any of us clueless bozos to accomplish anything on His behalf in the absolute sense. But for some reason, He has limited Himself to working through humans and their prayers. *This is that reason.*

That's why He tells us to pray for people and various things. Our prayers and obedience to His Word open the door for Him to act within our lives and those for whom we pray because we are operating in our God-given authority over the earth.

The Second Adam Won Back Dominion at the Cross

This is also the rationale behind the Incarnation of Jesus in human form — man had sinned, so it took a perfect Man (the Second Adam) to redeem us from our bondage to sin and its penalties. The New Testament says Jesus, as the sinless Man, regained that authority from the enemy through His death on the cross and subsequent resurrection 3 days later. As we read in earlier in this chapter:

> *So God raised him to the highest place. God made his name greater than every other name so that every knee will bow to the name of Jesus — everyone in heaven, on earth, and under the earth. And everyone will confess that Jesus Christ is Lord and bring glory to God the Father. — Philippians 2:9-11 NCV*

Jesus Restored Dominion to Believers

Jesus Himself states in the Great Commission:

> ***All authority has been given to Me in heaven and on earth.*** *Go therefore and make disciples…*
>
> *— Matthew 28:18-19a (emphasis mine)*

A well-known Bible teacher once said, "Whenever you see the word 'therefore,' you always have to look at the phrase before that to see what it's 'there for'!" In this instance, Jesus delegated His authority to us as believers.

> *…but as many as did receive him to them* ***he gave authority to become sons of God*** *— to those believing in his name*
>
> *—John 1:12 YLT (emphasis mine)*

The word "authority" in both these verses is the same Greek word *exousia* we discussed earlier. This means Jesus — and as believers, we — have been given authority which must be obeyed by those commanded.

The Epistles are filled with references to Satan's defeat by Jesus through His death and resurrection. Because we Christ-followers are God's adopted children and joint-heirs with Christ, we have authority over the devil and his minions to keep them from carrying out their assignments against those for whom we pray, including ourselves. James proclaims:

> *…God resists the proud, but gives grace to the humble. Therefore submit to God. Resist the devil and he will flee from you.*
>
> *—James 4:6-7*

Nowhere in the Word does it say, "Pray to God to get the devil off of us." Rather, it says as we are submitted to God (properly related to our governing authority), we receive His grace, and thus equipped, we are commanded to tell the devil to go away.

Before we move on, I want to emphasize a point here: because Jesus' name is superior to every other name in both the natural and spiritual realms, that means when we pray in that Name, those other names must submit to His authority and obey those who are invoking it in prayer.

- What is cancer? *It's a name.*
- What is heart disease? *It's a name!*
- What is diabetes? *It's a name!*
- What is HIV? *It's a name!*
- What is bipolar disorder? *It's a name.*
- What is financial lack? *It's a name!*
- What is addiction? *It's a name!*
- What is family strife? *It's a name!*
- What is divorce? *It's a name!*
- Who is Satan? *He's a name!*

And all those names must bow in submission and obedience to the precious name of Jesus when we believers pray in the authority He purchased for us in His death, burial, and resurrection!

We Are Not Helpless Victims!

So when bad things happen to us as believers, it is most often because we — not God — have permitted them to happen! This is one of the most dangerous aspects of the Calvinist/Catholic lie that we are helpless victims of God-authored sickness, lack, and calamity: *we never enforce our God-given authority over the devil and his works.*

There is another crucial implication to this passage: if we have uncon fessed/unrepented sin in our lives, our authority over the devil is precisely ZERO. Why? Because whenever we are in rebellion against

God's kingdom, we are playing on Satan's turf, not His. In such circumstances, *we cannot not exercise authority over Satan's kingdom because we are in fact submitted to it.*

Those who know me well know I'm a huge Tolkien fan. I've read *The Hobbit* and *The Lord of the Rings* trilogy multiple times, I own all the movies, and I used to play *Lord Of The Rings Online* (lotro.com), a MMRPG based upon the novels.

My absolute favorite scene from *The Lord Of The Rings* movie trilogy is the one where Gandalf confronts the Balrog in the Mines of Moria during *The Fellowship Of The Ring.* He strikes his staff on the bridge and shouts with complete authority:

YOU SHALL NOT PASS!!

I cannot think of a more apt portrayal of what prayer is all about!

When the devil comes against our families through sickness, poverty, disaster, etc., we stand on our delegated authority as sons of the Living God and boldly declare to the powers of darkness, "YOU SHALL NOT PASS!!" — and make it stick!

Example #1

Back in the late 1983, I was preparing to move from Mountain View, California in Silicon Valley to Tulsa, Oklahoma, to take on a new IT job there at a ministry. At first, I was a more than a little concerned about the whole tornado thing, something for which Oklahoma is justifiably infamous — I mean the National Severe Storm Center is in Norman, Oklahoma for an excellent reason!

One night before we moved, I had a dream in which I was standing in our California home's living room, looking out the front picture window at a large tornado crossing the playing field of the high school across the street. It was coming straight at the house. In that dream,

I literally saw a demonic face at the top of that tornado. I then spoke out in my authority as a believer, rebuking the tornado and commanding it to get away from our house in the name of Jesus. The tornado responded by making an immediate 90-degree turn to the right and continued in that direction, leaving our house undamaged. The dream ended with me waking up in wonder at what I had seen there.

Armed with the revelation God gave me in that dream, we confidently moved to Tulsa. Within the first few months, a major tornadic storm system hit the city. I stood praying outside our apartment in the parking lot and saw several funnels form at various times. In each instance, I commanded them to stop in the name of Jesus and, without exception, they retracted into the cloud base — *not a single tornado touched the ground.* In the ensuing 16 years we lived in Tulsa and Wichita, Kansas, we repeatedly had storms producing tornadoes elsewhere in the vicinity, but near none of our homes.

You may dismiss this as mere coincidence, wishful thinking, or delusions of grandeur on my part. Say what you want, but I was there, and I saw the funnels not touch down!

Example #2

Another example is divine healing. I've lost count of the times I've prayed for healing for myself and others, and God has answered with miraculous demonstrations of His power.

One time, a close friend and former coworker in Reno, Nevada, was in a horrific car accident. When I later saw a recording of the newscast covering the wreck, her car looked like a giant had wadded it up like a ball of aluminum foil — it was a miracle that she survived at all!

She ended up in the hospital in a coma, and the prognosis was decidedly not good. I called my close friend and former pastor, Rev. David Oberg, who pastors a thriving church, Faith Alive! Christian Center, there in Reno and asked him to go pray for her since I was in Tucson and too far away to do so myself.

He went and laid hands on her, praying the prayer of faith for her complete recovery. Within a day or two, she came out of the coma. Within a month or so, they discharged her from the hospital . She is now completely recovered, with full use of her mental faculties.

David exercised his authority as a believer over the powers of darkness who had tried to destroy my friend and over the incredible damage inflicted upon her brain and body to save her life.

Conclusion

The bottom line is this: we Christ-followers are not helpless victims of a cosmic child-abusing God — or even the evil intentions of Satan, for that matter.

We have God-given authority as believers, not to order Him around, but to command the devil, his servants, and the forces of nature to obey us and stay away from our families, our jobs, our homes, and our finances.

CHAPTER

7

The Sovereignty of God's Word

IN THE PREVIOUS CHAPTER, WE DISCUSSED how God Almighty is indeed sovereign, but has self-limited His sovereignty through delegating of some of His authority to us as His children. We will now address the second way in which He has limited His own sovereignty: His promises, all of which are contained within His revealed will to humanity, the Bible.

The Virtue of Integrity

God's Word is incredibly important to Him. He has declared in multiple passages in both the Old and New Testaments that His Word is inseparable from Himself. In fact, in Chapter 1, the Gospel of John describes Jesus Christ as His Word in human form.

> *I will worship toward Your holy temple, and praise Your name For Your lovingkindness and Your truth; for* ***You have magnified Your word above all Your name.*** *— Psalm 138:2 (emphasis mine)*

We human beings value folks who keep their word to us and fulfill their promises. We especially honor those who do so despite opposition, adverse circumstances, and/or persecution.

We call them "people of integrity."

We also look down on those who betray our trust, those who, for various reasons, ranging from fear of consequences to mere inconvenience to outright laziness, decide they will not honor their promises or commitments. We intrinsically despise those who cheat on their wives, abscond with funds entrusted to their care, commit treason against their countries, show cowardice in the face of the enemy, or are abusers of the innocent/vulnerable — that is, *those who cannot be trusted.*

So we have an ingrained racial (mankind racial, not ethnic racial) belief/assumption that other humans should keep their word. I believe this comes from the verse in Genesis 2 where God said, "Let Us make man in Our image..." According to that verse, God created mankind with the intrinsic characteristics of His own being.

Newton's Third Law of Thermodynamics (the Law of Entropy) illustrates the truth of how nothing can spawn — or evolve into — something greater than itself. Therefore, we can safely conclude we silly humans didn't come up with this ingrained value for integrity on our own spin, but in fact our Creator imparted it to us. Indeed, the Living God values His own integrity so highly He ensured all of us silly humans possess a similar value for it, though societies suppress that innate sense through idolatry.

Why should we respect, honor, and submit to any god who cannot be trusted to keep his own word? Why should the One True Living God be exempt from His own standard?

The Bible also repeatedly states God is no respecter of persons, meaning that His Word is true and dependable for every man, woman, and child on the planet.

The one thing we can always take to the bank is the Word of God.

- We are what it says we are,
- We can have what it says we can have
- We can do what it says we can do
- We are going where it says we are going!

These are not subject to divine whim. Our God makes no arbitrary exceptions whenever He takes a notion to do so for reasons known only to Himself.

Yes, No & Wait

There's a very pious-sounding saying that has been running around the organized church for a few years now that goes something like this: "God answers our prayers with yes, no, or wait." While there is some truth to that saying, most Christians take the concept way outside of its scriptural limits. Here's why I say this.

Yes

Jesus repeatedly promises us affirmative answers to our prayers, both directly and through His apostles. Just a few examples:

> *Yet you do not have because you do not ask. —James 4:2b*

> *For all the promises of God in Him are Yes, and in Him Amen, to the glory of God through us. — 2 Corinthians 1:20*

> *Now this is the confidence that we have in Him, that if we ask anything according to His will, He hears us. And if we know*

> *that He hears us, whatever we ask, we know that we have the petitions that we have asked of Him. — 1 John 5:14-15*
>
> *If you abide in Me, and My words abide in you, you will ask what you desire, and it shall be done for you. —John 15:7*
>
> *If you ask anything in My name, I will do it. —John 14:14*

So that's the "yes" portion. No problem so far.

Wait

Often there is a timing issue involved where God has already answered our prayers in the affirmative in the spirit realm, but He has certain circumstances to arrange here on earth or some character development He wants to complete in us before we see the manifestation of that answer.

Many times, our answers require other people to choose to do something good for us, perhaps something they don't initially want to do. Because they are limited to space and time (as we are), have limited insight and understanding (as we do), have their free will corrupted by sinful flesh in varying degrees (as we do), and may be deceived by satanic prejudices and emotional bondages (as we frequently are), they resist God's influence on our behalf, at least for a time.

On top of all that, as exemplified by the prophet Daniel, there is spiritual opposition to our answers being delivered to us, demonic powers who oppose the angels tasked with delivering our answer to us.

Sometimes, it's *all* of them.

Most people turn their "wait" into a "no" simply by giving up. They then shift the blame onto God by stating He said "no" when, in fact, the problem was their adopting an "add-water-and-stir" mentality towards the process. They then conflate their finite understanding of the situation and the Word by creating erroneous theology to explain why they are "right."

No

There are only two times when the Bible says we'll get a "no" answer to our prayers.

The first has to do with the passage in 1 John 5:14-15. We've just examined where it says our praying according to God's will causes Him to hear and answer us. Its corollary is if we pray over a matter opposed to the will of God, He neither hears nor answers.

The Epistle of James specifies the second one: when we ask selfishly for the fulfillment of our own flesh.

> *You ask and do not receive, because you ask amiss, that you may spend it on your pleasures. —James 4:3*

Many misinterpret this last verse as a blanket proscription against every prayer asking God to meet our needs, proclaiming with false piety, "It's selfish to pray for ourselves; we should pray for others." Yes, we are supposed to pray for others, but it's "both-and," not "either-or."

Such folks use this as an excuse to give up on their prayers for healing, financial assistance, or other personal issues, despite the Bible containing numerous promises where God specifically proclaims His willingness to meet those types of needs in our lives.

The Promises of God

Let's explore some of these promises, specifically ones concerning salvation, health/healing, divine protection, and financial provision.

Promises of Salvation

First, let's discuss salvation and what that entails. Many verses in the OT collectively predict how salvation would come to God's people, the Jews, as well as the Gentiles (the rest of mankind) through a Messiah Who would be born of a virgin in Bethlehem and suffer for the sins of the world. The NT contains even more verses collectively stating in no-uncertain-terms how salvation is by grace alone through faith alone in Christ alone, but these two sum it all up nicely:

> *...there is no other name under heaven given among men by which by which we must be saved. — Acts 4:12*

> *...that if you confess with your mouth the Lord Jesus and believe in your heart that God has raised Him from the dead, you will be saved. For with the heart one believes unto righteousness, and with the mouth confession is made unto salvation. — Romans 10:9-10*

No mature Christ-follower contests the Truth and validity of such verses. Indeed, all of us would shout, "Amen!!" to a proclamation how it is impossible to have a vital faith in the Person and finished work of Jesus Christ without accepting these verses as absolute Truth and acting on them.

Promises of Healing & Protection

However, the ballgame changes completely when we encounter such verses such as:

> *...Who Himself bore our sins in His own body on the tree, that we, having died to sins, might live for righteousness — by Whose stripes you were healed. — 1 Peter 2:24*

Those selfsame folks who would never question the first part of the verse as being subject to divine whim will immediate start waffling on the second half where it talks about healing, asking, "Well, what if it's not

God's will to heal me?" instead of taking Him at His clearly written Word it is indeed His will to heal us. In Psalms, it says:

> *No evil shall befall you, nor shall any plague come near your dwelling; for He shall give His angels charge over you, to keep you in all your ways. — Psalm 91:10-11*

Those who vociferously rise to defend the Truth of salvation in Jesus would say, "Well, God is sovereign and sometimes He lets evil come our way to teach us to be humble or to depend on Him," or some other such pious-sounding drivel. Again, why would God promise His angelic protection against evil and sickness if He will not do it?

Elsewhere in Psalms, you will find:

> *Bless the Lord, O my soul; and all that is within me, bless His holy name! Bless the Lord, O my soul, and forget not all His benefits: Who forgives all your iniquities, Who heals all your diseases, Who redeems your life from destruction, Who crowns you with lovingkindness and tender mercies, Who satisfies your mouth with good things, so that your youth is renewed like the eagle's. — Psalm 103:1-5*

Again, many would agree that God always "forgives all our iniquities," "redeems our lives from destruction," and "crowns us with lovingkindness and tender mercies," but when pressed on "heals all our diseases," they hem and haw over whether it is always God's will to heal us.

Promises of Financial Provision

Those selfsame folks would also erroneously say, "God doesn't give me any money to keep me humble" although God states He will not only meet our financial needs, but actually prosper us, dozens of times throughout both the Old and New Testaments. For one example, the following verse promises:

> *And God is able to make all grace (every favor and earthly blessing) come to you in abundance, so that you may always and under all circumstances and whatever the need, be self-sufficient — possessing enough to require no aid or support and furnished in abundance for every good work and charitable donation. — 2 Corinthians 9:8 AMP*

Some would explain this away as merely a spiritual blessing. But if you follow proper principles of hermeneutics, the context of this verse is a monetary offering, so applying this verse to finances is a perfectly — indeed the only — legitimate interpretation.

Am I the only one who sees a double-standard here?

Where's the Line?

Where can we safely draw the line between the promises where God will sovereignly honor His Word and those where He may take a notion to not honor them?

Frankly, *nowhere!*

Why?

Because it puts us squarely in the same seats as liberal theologians who water down the Word, using human reason to determine what part of God's Word is true and what isn't.

As finite, fallible — and mostly clueless — human beings, we don't have the freedom or the capability of making such distinctions.

We have only 2 choices:

1. Believe all of it, or;
2. Believe none of it!

CHAPTER

8

What Defines Suffering For Jesus?

WHENEVER STANDING ON GOD'S PROMISES for victory over the circumstances of life is being taught, folks from traditional churches and denominations will frequently counter with the objection, "Aren't we supposed to be suffering for Jesus' sake? Aren't we called to simply endure rather than fight them?"

Excellent question, thank you for asking!

Yes, there are indeed things we are called to suffer for Jesus' and/or righteousness' sake. This concept is clearly scriptural and mentioned throughout the New Testament. That being said, not everything we suffer qualifies.

However, in order to define what "suffering for Jesus" really is, we must also determine what it's not as well.

Basically, there are at least 9 general classifications of suffering:

1. Suffering caused by our own sinful choices
2. Suffering caused by the sinful choices of others
3. Suffering caused by natural disasters
4. Suffering caused by disease
5. Suffering caused by accidents
6. Suffering caused by demonic attack/oppression
7. Suffering caused by self-sacrificial choices to the benefit of one or more other human beings.
8. Suffering caused by crucifying one's own fleshly desires out of loving obedience to Jesus
9. Suffering caused by persecution because we are — and are known to be — Christ-followers

To determine which of these sufferings qualifies as "suffering for Jesus' sake," we first have to determine who experiences what types of suffering and what — if anything — distinguishes that group from everyone else on the planet. In the first 6 cases, these types of suffering are universal to all mankind, so those who are suffering from any of these by definition cannot be suffering for Jesus' sake. #7 is in a gray area between the first 6 and the last 2; it can fall on either side depending on the circumstances.

Why?

Because any human being on the planet can do it, whether a Christian or not!

Crucifying Our Fleshly Desires

Jesus has commanded only Christ-followers to crucify their fleshly passions. The lost have exempted themselves from His directive because they are already in rebellion against the Most High. Crucifying our flesh means we have resisted — by God's grace — our selfish desires/ tendencies and chosen to lovingly obey God by serving Him and others. Anyone who has overcome an addiction knows this battle with sinful self intimately, but addicts are not some kind of special case. The suffering experienced as we crucify our fleshly desires in order to serve Him and others is the normal Christian life described throughout the New Testament. As one of my favorite preachers has said on many occasions, "Never pass up a good opportunity to die!"

Persecution

As for persecution, only those who have been born from above by submitting to His Lordship are eligible to suffer for His name's sake. This means that, because we have publicly proclaimed our faith in the Lord Jesus Christ, another someone or a group of someones has determined to harm us in some form or fashion. Such harm can range from the trivial (hurling verbal or written insults) to the heinous (torture and death) and everywhere in between..

What Does Not Qualify as Persecution

Please note if you are constantly late to work, doing poor quality work, taking long lunches, consistently leaving before quitting time, and are using work time to "witness" to your coworkers and then get fired, that is not persecution for righteousness' or Jesus' sake; you are reaping what you've sown through your wretched work ethic.

Please further note that if people reject you and refuse to socialize with you because you are an obnoxious horse's patootey, you are not suffering for Jesus' sake; you are reaping the crop of rejection you have sown through your antisocial behaviors.

As a final example, if you physically and/or sexually abuse your spouse and children while claiming to be Bible-believing Christian who is obeying God, and later get arrested, tried, and convicted for domestic violence, incest, and other charges, your sentence is not persecution for righteousness' sake — you have committed heinous crimes and received your just punishment for them.

Persecution for righteousness' sake means you are a follower of Jesus Christ and have been somehow penalized for that fact alone!

Frankly, American believers are a bunch of wimps compared to our foreign brethren.

- We whine whenever atheists and liberals portray us as religious nut-cases because we actually believe the Bible.
- We lament when mocked for proclaiming the Lord is worthy of our devotion, obedience, and worship.
- We complain when scorners ridicule us for daring to take a stand against the sacrifice of babies on the altar of their mothers' selfish convenience.

Truthfully, we haven't even begun to suffer persecution — yet!

Islam

In every Moslem country I can think of, if you convert to Christianity and publicly show your conversion by being water baptized, the chances are extremely high — approaching certainty — your own relatives will murder you in an honor killing without them facing criminal prosecution afterwards. If your family doesn't kill you, then the government will execute for violating the state religion of Islam and *sharia* law. The nightly news rarely if ever reports this because it doesn't serve the inexplicably pro-Moslem bias of the liberal media.

China

In China (yes, the selfsame China which produces most of our day-to-day purchases), they baptize believers by immersion in raw sewage after imprisoning them, not to mention beatings, deprivations, and other tortures.

If the government decides you are becoming too much of a nuisance, they'll put a bullet in your brain and send your family the bill for the ammunition expended. They do not report this on the nightly news because that doesn't serve the liberal media's agenda, either. After all, China is a socialist utopia where everyone is happy, healthy, prosperous, and free — NOT!

You might accuse me of exaggerating, but these are daily occurrences in such countries, as documented in *Jesus Freaks*, a book ghostwritten back in the 1990s by Dr. LeAnna Eldridge of Life Christian University for the band DC Talk. Other credible Christian ministries, such as Voice of the Martyrs, also document such persecution.

What does the Word say about such suffering? Jesus said:

> *Remember the word which I said to you, A slave is not greater than his lord. If they persecuted Me, they also will persecute you. —John 15:20*

> *Blessed are those who are persecuted for righteousness' sake, For theirs is the kingdom of heaven. Blessed are you when they revile and persecute you, and say all kinds of evil against you falsely for My sake. Rejoice and be exceedingly glad, for great is your reward in heaven, for so they persecuted the prophets who were before you. — Matthew 5:10-12*

The Apostle Paul wrote:

> *All who desire to live godly in Christ Jesus will suffer persecution. — 2 Timothy 3:12)*

Folks, that is just as much of a promise in the Word of God as:

...by His stripes we were healed. — 1 Peter 2:24b

Many of the saints in the early church were tortured and executed at the behest of corrupt Roman emperors such as Nero and Domitian. They considered it an honor to experience such a thing because of their love for the Lord. A corrupt and godless Catholic Church tortured and killed hundreds of thousands more, especially during the Protestant Reformation.

These saints were tortured, burned alive, beheaded, boiled in oil, attacked and eaten by wild beasts, and a host of other horrible, disgusting, and cruel treatments at the hands of their persecutors. Most of them died singing hymns of praise to our Lord.

Many of our modern brethren suffering persecution in Moslem and Communist countries exhibit similar courage and behaviors.

Now *that* is suffering for Jesus' sake!

CHAPTER

9

Temptations, Trials & Tribulations

IN THE PREVIOUS CHAPTER, WE DISCOVERED how not every negative circumstance in our lives meets the standard of "suffering for Jesus' sake" unless it arises from the denial of our flesh in obedience to Christ or persecution for our faith.

In this chapter, we will tackle head-on how God leverages all negative circumstances in our lives to mature us spiritually.

Verses appear throughout the New Testament, declaring how God uses such things to produce Christ-likeness in us and to develop our faith. For example:

> *'My brethren, count it all joy when you fall into various trials, knowing that the testing of your faith produces patience. But let patience have its perfect work, that you may be perfect and complete, lacking nothing.' —James 1:2-4*

However, later on in the selfsame chapter, James states:

> *'Let no one say when he is tempted, "I am tempted by God"; for God cannot be tempted by evil, nor does He Himself tempt anyone.' —James 1:13*

Sounds like a contradiction, right? But these two concepts are not at all antithetical. Here's why: just because God didn't cause them doesn't mean He can't use them.

tempted (*peirazo*)

> *to try, make trial of, test: for the purpose of ascertaining his quality, or what he thinks, or how he will behave himself*
>
> *to try or test one's faith, virtue, character, by enticement to sin*
>
> *to solicit to sin, to tempt*
>
> *of God:* ***to inflict evils upon one in order to prove his character and the steadfastness of his faith***

I think this pretty well puts paid to the claims of those who proclaim how God inflicts disaster folks to teach them something.

God is perfectly redemptive. We can experience the most corrupt, perverted, heinous, repulsive, and evil situations imaginable, but once we have submitted them to Him for healing and restoration, by His infinite knowledge, power, and love, He can — and does — bring good out of them. Astonishingly, He does this so perfectly, so seamlessly, it appears to us as if the whole thing as His will in the first place.

It's miraculous!

Case in point: the Holocaust. God, in no way, shape, or form, had anything to do with causing the Holocaust. That was Satan using his servants, Adolf Hitler, and assorted henchmen, to destroy God's covenant people. However, as ghastly and horrific as that monstrously evil event was, God redeemed it and used it to create the modern nation of Israel.

No matter how badly we bozo human beings mess things up, no matter how far we stray from His perfect will for our lives, God can and will take those sows' ears and make silk purses out of them. Yes, there will be consequences in this life we will experience because of the laws of sowing and reaping, but His mercy and lovingkindness will transform even them for our good.

What's a *Thlipsis?*

> *'These things I have spoken to you, that in Me you may have peace. In the world you will have tribulation; but be of good cheer, I have overcome the world.' — Matthew 16:33*

This is one of the most significant verses in the New Testament. First, Jesus states the things He has been saying should produce peace in us. He then confirms we will experience tribulation in this world. The English word "tribulation" is the Greek word *thlipsis*:

tribulation (*thlipsis*)

> *affliction, tribulation, persecution, trouble, pressure, distress*

He immediately follows this with a command to cheer up because He has overcome the world.

How We Grow

Why does God allow us to experience *thlipsis?*

Resisting and overcoming such situations by the Word and grace of God is the way Christ-followers grow in faith and develop the fruit of the Spirit.

Here's an analogy: when we were born physically, we possessed every bone, muscle, and organ we would ever have. However, we had no strength in them and no ability to control them. We had to have our heads supported because our spine and neck muscles were not strong enough to handle the weight of our heads.

As we started taking in nourishment, we began growing. As we grew, we instinctively started moving our bodies, opposing gravity, building strength in our muscles and bones. Eventually, we could turn ourselves over.

Later, we got up onto our hands and knees, then after a time crawled. After some more time doing that, we started standing up on our legs. After we developed our leg bones and muscles doing that for a bit, we began walking with the help of our parents and nearby furniture. As our sense of balance developed, we then walked unassisted, eventually started running, and then our moms went nuts trying to keep track of us!

When we experienced the New Birth, we were baby Christians with no strength, no knowledge, and no sense of balance. As we started off, we had this incredible feeling of cleanness and freedom, the forgiveness of our sins brought to us. We started delving into the Word, fellowshipping with other believers, praying, worshipping, and witnessing our experience of the goodness of God.

As our walks with God progressed, eventually the feelings died out and Satan attacked us, trying to get us to doubt our salvation. If someone had properly discipled us, we resisted that attack with the Word of God, declaring Scripture verses promising us salvation, such as Ephesians 2:8-10 and Romans 10:9-10, etc. as well as appropriating the grace of God. Eventually, we were victorious against that attack and we no longer doubted our salvation — and indeed probably never will again for the duration of our time on earth.

Satan attacks us again.

We resist that attack, battling it by faith in God's Word and His grace.

We grow stronger.

Rinse and repeat.

Often, we fail — especially at first — and must ask God and others to forgive us. We then stand back up on our feet and resume the fight.

Over time, we fall less and less, becoming more and more balanced and experienced. All the while, just as a baby grows into a child, then a teenager, and finally an adult by resisting gravity with its muscles and exercising its mind, we oppose thlipsis, developing our faith muscles and renewing our minds in Christ by the Word until we reach spiritual adulthood.

So even though God doesn't cause *thlipsis* in our lives, He is more than willing and able to use it to grow us into mature adult believers. What is the fruit of all this?

> *'…love, joy, peace, longsuffering, kindness, goodness, faithfulness, gentleness, self-control…' — Galatians 5:22-23*

as well as faith in Him and His Word.

God somehow ensures that we are never over-matched in all this. He:

> *'…will not allow you to be tempted beyond what you are able, but with the temptation will also make the way of escape, that you may be able to bear it.' — 1 Corinthians 10:13b*

Every trial we face is small enough for us to face, yet large enough that we cannot face it alone in our own strength apart from His grace, love, Word, and our fellow Christ-followers.

His Grace is Sufficient!

Awhile back, God led me to explore the Greek words where Paul quotes Jesus in 2 Corinthians 11 as saying to him,

> *'My grace is sufficient for you, for My strength is made perfect in weakness.' — 2 Corinthians 11:9a*

When you dig into the Greek, it reads more like this:

> *'My merciful lovingkindness and holy influence provide you with unfailing strength and defenses, and complete contentment because I freely give you My might, My power to perform miracles, My ability to produce moral excellence, My resources for financial prosperity, as well as the military might of the angels of heaven fighting on your side. These gifts are all brought to fullness and completion amid your moral, mental, and physical weakness, your inability to understand yourself and others, and your failure to accomplish goals, endure trials, and resist temptation.' — 2 Corinthians 11:9a*

No matter how you cut it, it's about Him and His ability, not us and ours. No matter what the trial, temptation, tribulation, disaster, addiction, attack, or loss,

> *'...we are more than conquerors through Him who loved us!' — Romans 8:37*

He's given us the grace, the authority, the Word, and the blood of Christ to be *victors*, not victims.

CHAPTER

10

A Semi-Scholarly Analysis of the Book of Job

WHENEVER YOU START DECLARING HOW God doesn't visit disaster upon His children to teach them humility or some other lesson, frequently the first objection people trot out is the objection, "Well what about Job?"

Almost without exception, however, such folks have little concept about what that book actually says. Usually it's only second-hand information they have received from poorly researched sermons preached from a traditional (usually Calvinist) perspective.

Most believers are under the mistaken impression Job was some sort of prophet and then casually toss around cherry-picked verses with a total disregard for their context without knowing much of anything about the man and his story other than his horrific trials. This lack of understanding about this book is what causes so many problems.

But here is, as Paul Harvey used to say, *"the rest of the story!"*

A Brief Overview of Job

According to Bible scholars, Job lived during what theologians call the "patriarchal period" between when Adam and Eve were expelled from Eden and the appearance of Abraham. This timing issue is significant.

Why?

Because it predates the existence of any recorded covenant relationship between the One True God and His creation, man.

Furthermore, Job had no Scriptures. The first written books of the Bible were penned by Moses during the wilderness phase of the Exodus centuries later. In Job's day, only oral traditions existed.

These two facts are crucial because they show how, according to the biblical record,

- Job had almost no revelation of the One True God beyond His existence, His general displeasure with sinful behavior, and His acceptance of animal sacrifices as a temporary atonement for sins.
- God had not promised Job anything he could stand on in faith.
- Job knew nothing about the existence of the spirit realm (the alternate "dimension" where God and His angels, as well as Satan and his demons, exist).
- Job appears to be completely ignorant of Satan's existence.
- Also, because he lived several millennia prior to the life, death, and resurrection of Jesus, Job was unregenerate. That means he had never experienced the New Birth and therefore did not have the Holy Spirit dwelling inside his physical body, as all Christ-followers do. As a result, he had no spiritual authority against the devil to prevent such tragedies as the ones that befell him.

- Nowhere in the Bible does it describe Job as a prophet or priest empowered by calling and equipped by revelation to speak *ex officio* for God to other human beings.
- On top of that, all of his so-called "friends" were in precisely the same boat. !

To summarize what we know about Job:

- He was a righteous man (God said that Himself, so that is not debatable).
- He didn't have a covenant with God as Abraham and his descendants did, and we do today.
- He didn't have any Scriptures wherein God had promised or even revealed anything to him.
- He apparently didn't have a clue about the existence of angels, Satan, or demons.
- He was neither called nor empowered to speak on God's behalf to anyone
- He had not received the New Birth, therefore had no indwelling of the Holy Spirit within his physical body.
- He, therefore, had little or no spiritual authority on the earth.

Other Popular Misconceptions

Many have mistakenly assumed Job's trials went on for years. Actually, it all transpired over the course of only a few days or weeks, depending upon how much Job and his idiotic friends said which was not included in the book, as well as how long the pauses were between Job's rants and their responses.

Another popular abuse of this book comes from those who have created their own personal disasters through their own sins (selfishness, greed, hatred, lust, etc.). I've lost count of the jail inmates I've heard state they were like Job when they were going through nothing of the sort at all. They were in jail pending trial because they had committed one or more crimes (in other words, they were unrighteous), whereas Job was attacked despite the fact God had declared him righteous.

Truly Reported vs. Truly Spoken

As a result, the Book of Job has to be the most misunderstood, most misinterpreted, most misquoted book in the entire Bible!

I cringe every time I hear someone unctuously and ignorantly quote Job 1:21 after some disaster, like a child dying or other loss of a loved one, saying, "the Lord giveth, and the Lord taketh away; blessed be the name of the Lord". There is even a popular contemporary worship tune where it says, "He gives and takes away" during the song's bridge.

There's one major problem with doing this. *Job was dead wrong!*

"But wait!" you exclaim. "It says that right there in the Bible!"

Absolutely true; I am not contesting that fact in the slightest. Job indeed said those exact words. But the foundational doctrine of the verbal inspiration of the Scriptures in the original languages and their total infallibility does *not* extend to every word some unregenerate human said in it.

In other words, the Bible truly and factually reports what was said by everyone quoted, but not every word spoken by some of those folks was true and factual.

For example, sometimes the Bible quotes someone who was lying, such as Annanias and Sapphira in the Book of Acts. Elsewhere in that same book, Simon the Magician asked to buy the ability to perform miracles by the Holy Spirit. It would be ludicrous to assert Annanias and Sapphira's lies were the voice of God speaking through them, wouldn't it? Or that God inspired Simon ask to buy the ability to perform miracles?

But we accept the Bible is absolutely accurate in its reporting of those incidents — what was said by whom and the events which transpired. Why would we hold the words of any other human — other than Jesus or a prophet speaking *ex officio* from the Lord — to a different standard?

Not to mention the context of any quote made by any human being in the Bible also must be considered.

So we can safely conclude the Bible is 100% accurate and true in reporting what Job and those around him said. It is also completely accurate to say Job and his so-called buddies were mostly clueless about what they were talking about!

A Brief Synopsis of the Book of Job

Introduction

Chapter 1 describes Job as a righteous man and extremely blessed. He had 10 children, a huge servant staff, and extreme wealth. I guess you could say the Bible describes him as a patriarchal type of Warren Buffett or Jeff Bezos, fabulously wealthy and famous throughout the region.

Satan's First Attack

Verse 6 describes Satan entering God's presence. It's hard for us humans to get our puny minds wrapped around how our holy God would countenance the personification of evil in His presence, but that is precisely what this verse says, so it has to be The Truth.

Here we have yet another major distinction between Job and any Christ-follower at any time throughout history. The Hebrew word for Satan here is not his name, but his title. Here is how the Hebrew lexicon defines it:

satan

adversary, one who withstands

The Book of Revelation calls him the "Accuser of the Brethren."

> *Then I heard a loud voice saying in heaven, "Now salvation, and strength, and the kingdom of our God, and the power of His Christ have come,* ***for the accuser of our brethren, who accused them before our God day and night, has been cast down.***
>
> — *Revelation 12:10 (emphasis mine)*

This verse also describes the differentiation I am trying to describe here. Back in Job's day, Satan indeed had access to the presence of God to prosecute all of mankind before the throne. The basis of those accusations was sin. Because all have sinned (Romans 3:23), there was no viable defense any human could present to counter his accusations.

The finished work of Jesus destroyed both Satan's access to God as well as his power over us through sin, guilt, and shame. The New Testament epistles repeatedly reinforce this crucial concept by recounting Jesus' surpassing victory over Satan through the Cross and His resurrection. Thus, our accuser was cast down (the same term used when Jesus cast out demons). Bottom line? Satan no longer has our sins as evidence to wield against us in the heavenly courtroom.

All Satan has left is a single tool: *deception.* Since Jesus Himself called him the Father of Lies (John 8:44), we can safely assume he has an otherwise insurmountable mastery of them. That mastery can only be overcome by the power of God's Word, the grace of God, and the revelation and power of the Holy Spirit Who indwells all believers.

Back to Job

God then says something interesting to Satan about Job. He asks if he has "considered" Job. Most preachers interpret that as meaning God was bragging on Job to Satan.

However, when you look up the word "considered" in a Hebrew lexicon, you find it's the word *siym*. Interestingly enough, there are other definitions besides "considered" found there, like "to lay violent hands on" and so on. In the context of subsequent events which transpired, I believe it would be far more accurate to say God was accusing Satan of hatching some sort of evil plot to destroy Job.

Then Satan appears to get permission from God to attack Job. Could there be an alternate interpretation?

I believe there is. Take a quick glance at where Job says,

> *For the thing I greatly feared has come upon me, And what I dreaded has happened to me. —Job 3:25*

The idea Job was operating in fear rather than faith is bolstered by the description of his behaviors in verse 5. God answers Satan in verse 12 in an unusual way. He doesn't overtly give Satan permission, but says, *"Behold, all that he has is in your power..."*

Is it possible God was saying words to the effect of, "You already have power over him" due to Job's fear? But God did limit Satan to not touch Job's physical body.

We see what then happened: Job lost all his children and all his wealth.

Job's response was to not blame God and get bitter, something those casually quoting his book should note. Though he incorrectly attributed the catastrophes to God rather than Satan, God doesn't hold his ignorance against him and states Job remained blameless and without sin.

Satan's Second Attack

Chapter 2 begins with the same scene portrayed in Chapter 1: God is holding court and Satan shows up. God again asks the devil if he has "considered" Job.

This brings up a translational issue because the word for "considered" here differs from the one used in the previous chapter. Instead of the Hebrew word *siym*, the word used in verse 3 is *leb*, which — besides "considered" also means "heart", an "inclination", a "determination of will", among others. It would be safe to state, given the context, that God was asking Satan, "Have you truly set your heart on destroying Job?"

Again, God does not necessarily give Satan permission, but simply states that, "he is in your hand." Again I have to ask: Is God giving permission or did Job already give the devil an opening through his fear?

Regardless, the result was Job found himself in severe pain. His embittered wife chimes in and exhorts Job to "curse God and die," probably blaming God and/or Job in her grief for the demise of their children.

Again, Job incorrectly attributes the evil which came his way to God, and still He doesn't hold Job accountable for his ignorance of the facts — He declares Job righteous yet again.

Then Job's "friends" show up. What a bunch of ignorant losers! If you ever need exemplars for how *not* to minister to folks who are hurting, these are your boys.

Job Holds a Pity Party

In Job 3, Job now feels sorry for himself, whining to his friends. Frankly, if any of us were in the shape he was in and going through what he was going through, I don't think any of us would do much better, even with our being able to appropriate the grace of God. Almost all of us would be whimpering and most of us would blame God and be angry/bitter at Him for being "unfair" and a bunch of similar nonsense.

Job's "Friends" Accuse Him & Job Defends Himself

In Job chapters 4–37, we have a tedious exchange of arguments between Job and his so-called "friends" in which they play the blame game, accusing him of messing up and offending God somehow, so he needs to 'fess up and repent. Job responds by defending his own righteousness.

The friends' comments are a veritable litany of "man's religion." It is also crucial to note their complete lack of empathy and compassion towards Job. Everything they said was an exercise in blameworthiness.

God Shows Up & Sets the Record Straight

I love God's opening remarks to these sorry excuses for theologians:

> *Who is this who darkens counsel by words without knowledge?*
> *—Job 38:2*

God is telling the lot of them they are all desperately in search of a clue and then goes on for two chapters declaring exactly Who He is and who they aren't. At the beginning of Job 40, He then addresses Job personally and takes him to task for his words.

An interest item shows up later during God's questioning of Job:

> *Then I will also confess to you that your own right hand can save you. —Job 40:14*

Frankly, I'm at a loss concerning what exactly God is saying here. Could Job have prevented his catastrophes by refusing to indulge in fear? Could it be Job had a revelation of some sort of spiritual authority unspecified in the text and unused by him to turn events around?

No one on this side of heaven knows the answer to that question.

Wrapping Up

God finishes His discourse at the end of Job 41. In the opening verses of the following chapter, Job repents of his intemperate words.

God then rebukes Job's friends and tells them to offer a burnt offering of bulls and rams in the presence of Job, that he would then pray for them, and they would then be forgiven. I think it safe to say God was taking them to task for their complete lack of compassion for Job

When Job prayed for his friends (please note the power of forgiveness at work here; see Chapter 15), it says Job was restored double what had been taken from him; he had ten more kids and his daughters were some of the hottest babes around.

In Summary

James, the brother of Jesus, wrote in his epistle:

> *Indeed we count them blessed who endure. You have heard of the perseverance of Job and seen the end intended by the Lord — that the Lord is very compassionate and merciful. —James 5:11*

This, to me, puts the ultimate *coup de grâce* to the notion God visited evil upon Job, even passively. It echoes the saying generation after generation of God's people in the Old Testament said when they were worshipping God in the beauty of holiness:

> *Oh, give thanks to the Lord, for He is good! For His mercy endures forever! — 1 Chronicles 16:29*

God is a good God! And the devil is a bad devil!

CHAPTER

11

Praying According to God's Will

NOW, LET'S LAY ANOTHER KEY brick in our foundation for prayer: establishing God's will concerning whatever we will pray over. Our keynote passage for this chapter is:

> *Now this is the confidence that we have in Him, that if we ask anything according to His will, He hears us. And if we know that He hears us, whatever we ask, we know that we have the petitions that we have asked of Him. — 1 John 5:14-15*

Here it is again in the Amplified Version:

> *And this is the confidence (the assurance, the privilege of boldness) which we have in Him: [we are sure] that if we ask anything (make any request) according to His will (in agreement with His own plan), He listens to and hears us. And if (since) we [positively] know that He listens to us in whatever we ask, we also know [with settled and absolute knowledge] that we have [granted us as our present possessions] the requests made of Him. — 1 John 5:14-15 AMP*

One of the biggest fears concerning prayer among the untaught is a question something like, "What if I pray for something that isn't God's will?" The obvious answer, of course, is a corollary of the verse we've just read: God will not answer prayers that are not in agreement with his will.

That is a given.

However, I feel this is the wrong question at the outset.

Why? Because

- It is a question borne of fear rather than faith, and;
- It is a dead-end, leaving us with no path upon which to move forward.

Personally, I believe the real question is: "How can I pray prayers in agreement with the will of God and therefore receive what I am praying for?"

God's Word *is* His Will

This is not rocket surgery, folks: if you can find something God has promised in His Word, that *is* His will, period, end of story.

Whenever we pray in agreement with His Word — or better yet, actually pray His Word — we will always, at all times, in all places, and under all circumstances be praying the will of God.

One of my favorite quotes is one from the late missionary evangelist T. L. Osbourne who said,

> *"It is impossible to boldly claim by faith a blessing which we are not sure God offers, because the blessings of God can be claimed only where the will of God is known, trusted, and acted upon."*

This is a massively profound statement, so let's unpack it a bit: The first half simply states that for us to "boldly come to the throne of grace," we need to *know* — not guess, not kinda-sorta-maybe think, not hope something our pastor/parents/etc. taught us years ago, but *know with certainty* God has promised what we are about to pray for. The second half explains why: the will of God has to be known, trusted, and acted upon.

So before we can boldly come before the throne of grace, we need to do the following:

- Discover what God's Word says on the matter.
- Develop our faith in those verses.
- Incorporate them into our prayers.
- Act upon what we find in them.

If you ever attended one of our church's weekly prayer meetings whenever I was present, you would have heard me quoting God's Word extensively as I prayed for people — and even when I wasn't directly quoting Scripture, it would still have a solid biblical foundation. This ensured that whatever I was praying was indeed in agreement with God's will without question.

God's Universal Will

This is God's will for everyone who has submitted to the lordship of Christ. For example, it is always His will to:

- Save us when we receive Jesus as Lord
- Forgive our sins when we confess them to Him
- Redeem our mistakes, though we may suffer natural consequences for our actions

- Redeem the mistakes and sins inflicted upon us by other people
- Give us His peace surpassing our human comprehension
- Speak to us by the Holy Spirit through His Word, His voice within us, and the gifts of the Spirit
- Give us His wisdom when we lack it and ask for it
- Mold us into Christ-likeness through the renewing of our minds
- Have constant fellowship with us
- Give us abundance of grace
- Bless us whenever we obey Him
- Receive our worship, praise, and thanksgiving
- Heal our bodies from sickness and disease
- Heal our minds from the aftermath of trauma caused by abuse, neglect, and tragedy
- Restore our broken relationships
- Deliver us from the temptations and schemes of the devil
- Provide for our financial needs according to His riches in glory by Christ Jesus
- Reveal His will to us concerning things not specifically covered in His Word
- Minister life to the broken, hurting, and lost through us

You may consider some of that list a bit controversial, especially the items concerning healing and finances. But there are many verses that, when taken in context, specifically promise those things to us.

Don't take my word for it — look them up for yourself!.

The point here is this: we need to be digging into the Word and discovering for ourselves what God has accomplished in the death, burial, and resurrection of Christ, what He has imparted to us at the moment of salvation when we surrendered our lives to Him, and what He has promised us as believers under the New Covenant in Jesus' blood. The ongoing renewal of our minds by the Word of God is crucial to an effective prayer life!

The Specific Will of God for Each of Us

There are many issues we face in life where we do not have a specific revelation in God's Word concerning a matter. For example, should we:

- Accept a job opportunity offered to us
- Marry a specific someone we are attracted to
- Relocate to a new community for whatever reason
- Join a church or change churches
- Buy a house, car, or other major purchase
- Make a financial investment
- Have a baby or foster/adopt a child
- Any other major life decision
- Are unsure of God's timing for any of the items above
- And so on...

It is only in such cases when we should ever utter the words, "Lord, if it be your will." This is what James was talking about in his epistle when he admonishes,

> *Come now, you who say, 'Today or tomorrow we will go to such and such a city, spend a year there, buy and sell, and make a profit'; whereas you do not know what will happen tomorrow.*

> *For what is your life? It is even a vapor that appears for a little time and then vanishes away. Instead you ought to say, 'If the Lord wills, we shall live and do this or that.' But now you boast in your arrogance. All such boasting is evil.* —*James 4:13-16*

This passage is chastising believers for indulging in self-lordship.

Who are we to be determining our own courses of action without consulting the Lord and asking for His guidance and wisdom? Whenever we face these situations — and indeed we will — what we should do is seek God's will about them, asking the Holy Spirit to guide and direct us with His wisdom. Then, after He reveals His will concerning a situation, we can strongly pray in agreement with it.

Where God Guides, He Provides

God never leads us in a given direction and then leaves us hanging without the means — financial and otherwise — to get the job done. For example, as my wife and I took our desire to move into our current house to Him, we prayed God would lead us to the right house in the right location at the right price at the right time. Then we looked, avoiding hardening of the categories, allowing God to direct us. Once we discovered where He was leading us, we then prayed fervently in agreement with His will.

You know how we ended up buying a house in the high desert of Northern Arizona? My wife and I started out by looking for a larger apartment in Tucson, a good 5-hour drive south of here.

When we began, we thought all we could do was rent. As we walked out our search process, we discovered to our delight we actually could buy instead. After we looked fruitlessly for houses to buy in Tucson, the Lord led us to visit our current town, and on the fourth look, we found a really nice house for the amount we could afford — a place far newer and in a much nicer neighborhood than any of the houses we had looked at in Tucson for the comparable price.

We then prayed for our offer to be accepted. It was. We also prayed for favor with the mortgage company, that God would reveal any problems with the new place through the various inspections, the closing would go without a hitch, and we would have a smooth, incident-free move to our new digs. All those prayers were answered, but one: the mortgage broker missed the closing date by a day, so it caused us some personal and financial inconveniences. But everything else went perfectly!

The Religious Escape Clause

I have grown heartily fed up hearing well-meaning, but scripturally ignorant Christians pray for someone's needs, such as healing or financial provision, and somewhere along the line throw in what has been called The Religious Escape Clause: "Lord, if it be your will."

Some of you might bristle a bit at this point because you have tacked this phrase onto your own prayers for someone on one or more occasions, and I've just described you as "scripturally ignorant." Please cool your jets — I said "ignorant," not "stupid." Ignorance simply means someone has not been taught something. It might surprise you to discover out this phrase appears only twice in the Bible.

The first instance is in the Garden of Gethsemane, where Jesus is praying to the Father concerning His imminent trial, torture, and execution. Remember the types of prayer I described in Chapter 2? What He prayed was a prayer of consecration where He is submitting His future to the will of the Father.

At no time during this event, as recorded in any of the gospels, is Jesus praying for someone or something. If that were the case, it would have fallen into the category of a prayer of intercession or supplication, respectively. Let me hasten to point out that Jesus' prayer recorded in

John 17 took place in the upper room where they had the Last Supper, *not* at Gethsemane.

The second instance is the one in James we just discussed a couple of pages ago. Even then, since prayer is involved in our submission to God and seeking His will, we can stand upon His promises to guide and direct us and provide us with His wisdom.

If we are not determining God's specific will for our lives concerning something not clearly spelled out in His Word, or consecrating ourselves to His destiny for us, the phrase "if it be God's will" is not only not applicable, it's totally unscriptural.

Truth be told, it's a manifestation of personal unbelief, whether conscious or subconscious. In other words, the person saying it cannot bring him- or herself to believe something clearly promised in Scripture for whatever reason, shifting the blame to God in advance if it doesn't come to pass.

Selah!

CHAPTER

12

Praying in Faith

JUST ABOUT EVERY CHRISTIAN THEOLOGIAN can agree the following verse in the Book of Hebrews defines the concept of "faith:"

> *Now faith is the substance of things hoped for, the evidence of things not seen. — Hebrews 11:1*

As with almost all of my Scripture quotes, this one is from the New King James Version. Unfortunately, this and many other translations fail to do it translational justice. Here is the same verse in the Amplified Version, which does a far better job of interpreting the Greek:

> *Now faith is the assurance (the confirmation, the title deed) of the things [we] hope for, being the proof of things [we] do not see and the conviction of their reality [faith perceiving as real fact what is not revealed to the senses]. — Hebrews 11:1 AMP*

We receive *every* promise of God by faith. Therefore, it is crucial we understand both how faith works and how it relates to prayer. Let's unpack this verse a bit. The word "substance" in this verse is the Greek word *hupostasis*:

substance (*hupostasis*)

> *that which has foundation, is firm; that which has actual existence; a substance, real being; the substantial quality, nature, of a person or thing; the steadfastness of mind, firmness, courage, resolution; confidence, firm trust, assurance.*

Hupostasis means, by faith, the things we pray for have a tangible existence in the spirit realm (eternity) before they appear on Planet Earth.

The word for "evidence" is *elegchos*:

evidence (elegchos)

> *a proof; that by which a thing is proved or tested*

Elegchos is what they present in a court to prove to a judge or jury how thus-and-so-happened on such-and-such a date and time at the hand of whosoever.

All this means faith presents us with the tangible proof of what we have prayed for without our having seen it in the natural realm beforehand.

Faith's Foundation is Submission to God & His Word

Faith is a total dependency upon — and abandonment of control to — the Godhead and His Word to the exclusion of all others, including ourselves.

Faith is not a "leap" into the great unknown, but a measured step, based upon specific revelation from God's Word revealed by the Holy Spirit. The concept of a "leap of faith" is totally alien to the Bible and is completely unscriptural.

God does not respond to human need, only to faith in and submission to Him personally. There are millions in dire need throughout the world, the vast majority of whom refuse to submit to Jesus Christ as Lord of their lives because they have devoted themselves to false religions, such as Islam, Buddhism, and Hinduism, just to name three.

God will not answer prayers to these other so-called deities (e.g., Allah, Buddha, or Krishna, etc.) because that would establish them in wrong-doing (in these cases, idolatry), something He *never* does. If anyone actually receives answers to prayers made to these false gods, that is Satan answering so he can reinforce and perpetuate the lies they already believe.

Authority & Responsibility Must *Always* Be Equal

This is a fundamental truism of the universe.

- If a person has authority without being accountable for his or her actions, you have a dictator.
- If they do not give if a person the authority to get a job done, you have a scapegoat.

Here is another way of putting this: *whoever is in charge is responsible for the results.*

God never allows Himself to be held responsible for anything He is not in charge of. If we are not doing things according to His Word in the manner and with the attitudes expected of us, God is not bound to honor our prayers because we are in rebellion against His authority.

> ***Authority & responsibility must always be equal. Whoever is in charge is responsible for the results.***

Here is another fundamental truism: *a genuine test of submission only occurs when there is a difference of opinion.* Anyone can submit when he/she agrees with the boss. When the subordinate does what the boss wants anyway, with a respectful attitude, his/her submission becomes a proven fact rather than an idle intention.

True submission to God is evidenced in our lives whenever we want to do one thing, God wants us to do another, and we obey Him.

Let me be perfectly clear: this is not about our attempts to achieve perfection by our own dead religious works, but about an attitude and lifestyle of submission to the revealed will of God for our lives.

Faith is Allowing God to Control a Situation so His Results Will Prevail

We don't like this idea very much because our corrupt flesh cherishes "The Lie" perpetrated by Satan in Eden (you can be your own lord and it will work). The idea of abandoning control to an invisible, though loving, Being Who demands our total allegiance runs directly contrary to The Lie.

This is also how the Book of James can say "faith without works is dead." As we trust God, we also obey Him out of that faith. As God shows Himself faithful by blessing our obedience, we learn to trust Him even more.

Think in terms of a "victorious cycle" as opposed to a vicious one!

This is why "leaps of faith" are totally contrary to the Word. Some challenges are simply too big a bite for us to chew off in one gulp. We take steps of trust and obedience. This builds our faith and willingness to take the next step of faith. By this, God is building a track record of His faithfulness within our consciousness.

That's why many Scriptures talking about recounting the good works of God exist, exhorting us to bring them to remembrance in praise and thanksgiving. It reinforces our faith for the next step.

Faith is Not a Commodity

Many have taught faith is some sort of "thing" which can be obtained or lost.

[LOUD BUZZER] ***Sorry, wrong answer! Thank you for playing!***

Faith is relational, period. Therefore, it is based entirely upon our personal surrender to the Godhead:

- Through the lordship of Jesus Christ in our lives
- By His shed blood and finished work on the cross
- By the power of His resurrection from the dead
- By the presence and power of the Holy Spirit inhabiting our physical bodies
- As revealed in His written Word, the Bible
- As revealed by His Holy Spirit speaking into our lives through other mechanisms consistent with and subordinate to His written Word.

Christianity is about relationship, not religion.

The Bible is not an end unto itself. Its Author wrote it to lead us into an intimate personal relationship with Him. Our faith is in a Person, not a book. Anyone who teaches otherwise has missed the point completely!

The Book reveals who that Person is, how He operates, what He has said and done, what He expects from us, and what He has promised, both to those who follow Him and those who don't.

While our faith grows through a greater revelation of Who God is and what He has promised, it cannot diminish unless we choose to walk away from Him through apathy, unbelief, or rebellion.

Faith is a God-given Gift

> *For by grace you have been saved through faith, and that not of yourselves; it is the gift of God, not of works, lest anyone should boast. For we are His workmanship, created in Christ Jesus for good works, which God prepared beforehand that we should walk in them. — Ephesians 2:8-9*

In this passage, God tells us faith has saved us and this faith is not the result of our own efforts, desires, or accomplishments — it's a gift! The corollary to this truth is we have zero basis for drawing attention to ourselves for our great faith or any other aspect of our relationship with the Most High. He started the whole thing through the Person of His Son Jesus Christ in His life, death, burial, and resurrection. Even our ability to receive His incredible gift of salvation is by His grace opening up revelation of these things to us so we could respond to them.

So it is with prayer.

We pray by grace through faith and receive whatever God has promised by grace through faith, and we offer thanksgiving and praise back to Him by grace through faith.

Anyone who says otherwise is putting you under a system of works.

The Required Measure

> *For I say, through the grace given to me, to everyone who is among you, not to think of himself more highly than he ought to think, but to think soberly, as* ***God has dealt to each one a measure of faith.*** *— Romans 12:3 (emphasis mine)*

The word "measure" is the Greek word *metron*,

measure (metron)

> *measure, an instrument for measuring; a vessel for receiving and determining the quantity of things, whether dry or liquid; a graduated staff for measuring, a measuring rod; proverbially, the rule or standard of judgment; the required measure, the due, fit, measure*

This is a word describing some sort of vessel or stick used for measurement. A kitchen measuring cup and a yardstick would both qualify as "measures" under the first part of this definition.

Personally, I believe the operative definition here is at the end: *the required measure.* Using this definition, we can truthfully and accurately state that God has given us the required measure of faith.

Why does this make any never mind?

The answer is simple: we have this sin-based, flesh-ingrained tendency to view God through the lens of our own selfishness, where partiality holds sway. We all have favorite people, and we are favorably disposed to do nice things for them, as opposed to those we don't like. We erroneously presume that God operates on the same basis.

This verse also completely negates an excuse offered by pietists misquoting 1 Corinthians 12:9: "I guess God didn't give me the gift of faith."

One of the essential lies of hyper-Calvinism is that God has unconditionally and unilaterally predestined some for salvation and has left everyone else out in the cold in some sort of heavenly Chicken-of-the-Sea tuna commercial: *Sorry, Charlie, you're doomed!* To put it bluntly, it's salvation by cosmic lottery, not by faith.

God is totally impartial. He loves all of us equally, and we can extrapolate this concept to faith and prayer as well.

The Spiritual is Like the Physical

In Chapter 9, we discussed how our spiritual "muscles" develop by our opposing temptations, tribulations, and trials in the same way our physical muscles develop by opposing gravity.

Our job is to feed on the Word. We then oppose the negative circumstances and trials which come our way by faith in that Word, thus allowing our Heavenly Daddy to nurture and raise us into maturity.

Just as some people have developed their muscles more than others through training and discipline, so too are there Christians who have developed their "faith muscles" to a greater extent than other believers, also through training and discipline.

We all have the same faith potential given by the same impartial God and no one has any inherent advantage over his or her brothers and sisters in Christ.

Faith ≠ Denial

Many people accuse believers who stand in faith on God's promises, saying they are in denial of the situation.

Untrue!

Here is the difference between faith and denial:

- Denial is our refusal to accept something as factual. This is the essence of mind science and other cultic practices.
- Faith is our trust in God's character and promises as revealed in His Word, which trumps whatever we perceive with His higher reality.

So with an illness:

Denial says: "I'm not sick, I'm not sick, I'm not sick!"

Faith says: "By Jesus' stripes I'm healed!" (1 Peter 2:24)

We are not denying the fact we are sick, but are, in fact, declaring how God's Word supersedes that fact with the Truth of His healing power.

Faith, Not Sight

> *For we walk by faith, not by sight. — 2 Corinthians 5:7*
>
> *...being the proof of things [we] do not see and the conviction of their reality [faith perceiving as real fact what is not revealed to the senses]. — Hebrews 11:1b AMP*

This refines our concept of faith even further. Faith believes God's Word despite what we:

- Perceive with our senses (sight, smell, touch, taste, hearing)
- Comprehend with our intellect or intuition
- Feel with our emotions
- Consider as true or factual in this natural realm

God is a Good God!

> *Blessed is the man who endures temptation; for when he has been approved, he will receive the crown of life which the Lord has promised to those who love Him. Let no one say when he is tempted, "I am tempted by God"; for God cannot be tempted by evil, nor does He Himself tempt anyone. —James 1:12-13*

We've already explored in Chapter 9 how the word "tempted" in verse 13 is the Greek word *peirazo* which means in this context *"to inflict evils upon one in order to prove his character and the steadfastness of his faith."*

The bottom line here is this: faith always believes that God is the solution, *not* the problem.

God Has Already Provided What We Need

> *What then shall we say to these things? If God is for us, who can be against us? He who did not spare His own Son, but delivered Him up for us all, how shall He not with Him also freely give us all things? — Romans 8:31-32*

> *Grace and peace be multiplied to you in the knowledge of God and of Jesus our Lord, as His divine power has given to us all things that pertain to life and godliness, through the knowledge of Him who called us by glory and virtue, by which have been given to us exceedingly great and precious promises, that through these you may be partakers of the divine nature, having escaped the corruption that is in the world through lust. — 2 Peter 1:2-4*

Please note where it talks about God giving us something in the 2 Peter passage. *It is in the past tense.* Also, please note the fact we have "escaped" — also in the past tense — "the corruption that is in the world through lust." This means that, though we live in a corrupt and sinful world and struggle with our innately sinful flesh, we are not prisoners to their power.

Finally, check out the words "all things" in both passages. What gets excluded when we use the word "all?" "All things" means precisely that: *all things without exception.*

Faith considers what God has promised to be an already-accomplished fact in the spirit realm through the finished work of the cross and all we need to do is believe it despite:

- Lies of the devil to the contrary
- Advice to the contrary from carnally minded human beings, well-meaning or otherwise
- Reports by real and so-called "experts" to the contrary
- Perceived facts or diagnosed symptoms of the situation

Defense, Not Offense

Another implication of this idea is we are never struggling to get something we don't have, but are defending what God has already given to us from the spiritual psychopath (Satan) who is trying to steal it. Most people mistakenly think prayer is about convincing God to do something for us when in fact He's already done it and we are simply enforcing His will on the earth.

That's a completely different mind-set, now isn't it?

Doubts vs. Unbelief

Doubts

Doubts occur whenever our trust in God is challenged beyond our current comfort zone. Our puny minds are struggling to wrap themselves around whatever it is God has promised or commanded of us.

Doubts are not sinful.

As we've discussed in Chapter 9, doubts are to our faith, as gravity is to our bodies. In the same way we develop our physical muscles by opposing gravity, we develop our "faith muscles" by opposing our natural doubts. Condemning ourselves for doubts would be like us doing so for our inability to walk as an infant.

Unbelief

Unbelief is a sin we commit whenever we hear the revealed will of God for our lives and refuse to believe or obey. It is the essence of self-lordship, proclaiming we know better than God does on a given matter. That didn't fly in Eden and has never flown since.

Unbelief is at the core of the phrase, "I'll believe it when I see it!"

Our prime example of unbelief in action found in the Bible was the children of Israel during their exodus from Egypt. Starting on the banks of the Red Sea and continuing for another 9 challenges they faced after that, they refused to believe God's promises concerning His destiny for them (Promised Land, divine provision, victory in battle, etc.).

Instead, their constant mantra was, "You just brought us out here to die — we would have been better off back in Egypt!" or words to that effect. Finally, they received precisely what they had spoken: God confined that generation in the Sinai wilderness for 40 years, until they died off and the next generation could take up where their parents failed miserably.

You know how long it takes to cross the Sinai peninsula on foot? *About two weeks!*

Had those folks simply believed and obeyed the Word of the Lord, they would have been out of there within a month. But even during those 40 years in the wilderness, God provided for them supernaturally — food, water, shelter, warmth — even their clothes and sandals didn't wear out!

However, God doesn't permit us the privilege of looking down on them for their failures because we all have a tendency to do precisely the same thing! It is far easier to take a person out of slavery than to take slavery out of the person — our selfish flesh keeps wanting to return to its comfort zone of slavery to sin, rather than embracing our freedom in Christ Jesus.

This is why, barring human or divine intervention, the vast majority of abuse victims return to relationships with their original or other abusers — that's what they know and are used to. They are so used to mistreatment they don't know how to be in a healthy relationship.

Which then begs the question:

What in your life is "normal" that should not be?

Our Doubts Become Unbelief Only When We Speak Them

We can have doubts in our mind, yet still have faith in our hearts.

A fundamental truism of Christian counseling is this: if you listen long enough, your client will tell you exactly what is wrong with them. That is true because of the truths revealed in these two passages:

> *Brood of vipers! How can you, being evil, speak good things?* ***For out of the abundance of the heart the mouth speaks.*** *— Matthew 12:34 (emphasis mine)*
>
> *A good man out of the good treasure of his heart brings forth good; and an evil man out of the evil treasure of his heart brings forth evil.* ***For out of the abundance of the heart his mouth speaks.*** *— Luke 6:45 (emphasis mine)*

As with the children of Israel in the wilderness, whenever we declare with our mouths something in opposition to the revealed Word of God concerning the matter at hand, we are choosing to believe a lie rather than His Truth. We may have doubts concerning God's willingness and ability to deliver us screaming in our heads, but they do not become unbelief until and unless we give voice to them.

For example, when we face symptoms of illness,

Doubt says: "I'm struggling with this divine healing stuff. I feel terrible!"

Faith says: "By Jesus' stripes I'm healed!" (1 Peter 2:24)

Unbelief says: "God doesn't want to heal me. I'm going to die!"

Another example would be a financial challenge that is beyond our ability to handle using our own resources:

Doubt says: "I don't see how God will to meet our financial needs right now. The checkbook is empty!"

Faith says: "God supplies all my needs according to His riches in glory by Christ Jesus." (Philippians 4:19)

Unbelief says: "God doesn't care about us, we're going bankrupt!"

Our last example is a drug-addicted child of believing parents:

Doubt says: "My child's addiction is strong. I don't see how God is going to pull this one off."

Faith says: "My child is a disciple taught of the Lord and great is his/her peace and undisturbed composure." (Isaiah 54:13)

Unbelief says: "My child will die a horrible death from an overdose."

If you examine every instance where Jesus addressed His listeners as "you of little faith," He was talking to people who questioned God's willingness and ability to take care of them.

The Four Ps

Almost 50 years ago, right after I first got saved, I read a book in which the author described a process found throughout Scripture which he termed "The Four Ps," an acrostic describing God's dealings with His people. Here they are:

The Promise

This is whatever God has promised us as believers, starting with salvation and covering every area of our lives thereafter. There are two kinds of promises: positional and practical.

The Principle

What are God's conditions for receiving that promise?

- Positional promises: the requirement is simply accepting them by faith, believing they are true regardless of our previous experiences of neglect, abuse, and/or trauma, as well as our past and current sins and addictions.
- Practical promises: These build on those selfsame faith requirements, adding to them the requirement for us to engage in specific acts of obedience and/or changes of attitude over time.

The Problem

This is an opportunity to stand in faith on that promise, obeying the condition(s), with no external support, internal feelings, or perceived presence of God. "The Problem" comprises our earthly circumstances and the opposition of the powers of darkness, which are always opposed to whatever God says.

The burning question we deal with during The Problem is the same one Satan asked Eve in Eden — and it's the same folks asking it! — *"Has God said?"* The variants of that question are legion:

- "Did God really mean what He said?"
- "Is this really God's will?"
- "Is God making an exception for me because __________?" (fill in the blank)
- *ad infinitum, ad nauseam.*

We face a simple — though certainly difficult — choice: are we going to believe God's Word despite what our flesh, the world system, and the devil have to say on the matter, with no external evidence to support our faith other than the Word of God, or are we going to cave in and give up?

- Anyone can believe "by Jesus' stripes we're healed" when they are completely healthy, but how do we respond to a cancer diagnosis?
- It is absolutely no problem whatsoever to believe "God will supply our needs according to His riches in glory in Christ Jesus" when there's plenty of money in the bank to cover everything we need, but how do we respond when we were just laid off because the factory closed?
- It's easy to believe that God will protect us from the tongues of malicious gossips when everybody likes us, but will we really believe God and trust Him according to Isaiah 54:17 when people are doing their dead level best to discredit us with our employers or audiences?
- It's one thing to believe that Jesus has delivered us from the power of sin and that we are the righteousness of God in Christ (2 Corinthians 5:17) when we've lived a so-called "normal" life without becoming entrapped by any addictions. It's another thing altogether to believe that same promise while trying to climb out of the depths of a lifelong addiction to alcohol, drugs, tobacco, sex, or gambling.

Here is a fundamental truism concerning faith:

Our faith grows only when we face significant opposition over time, wielding only the Shield of Faith and Sword of the Spirit — the spoken Word of God — with no natural evidence to support that it's true.

That takes care of The Problem, now let's move on to…

The Provision

This is when the "whatever" God has promised manifests in our lives in this world

This is the awesome part, where we actually receive from God whatever it is we've been believing for. We've stood on the Word through thick and thin, weathered the attacks of the enemy upon our minds and lives, and we finally have in our hands the rewards for our faithful obedience to the Word.

This forms a valuable asset for facing future faith challenges called "experience." Someone said a long time ago, "a man with an argument is no match against a man with an experience." If you have experienced the healing power of God, or God's deliverance from a financial pickle, or He's pulled your irons out of the fire when people have attacked you unjustly, the most brilliant minds on the planet cannot pose a single argument which can talk you out of that experience.

As a former pastor once said, "You never really know that by Jesus' stripes you're healed until by Jesus' stripes you're healed!" Until you have the manifestation of your healing, such promises are like mathematical theorems awaiting their proofs.

Once you have an experiential revelation of God's will in a certain area, say healing, God has established a track record of being faithful to His Word in that same area. The next time you face a challenge concerning your physical health, finances, or whatever, those data points will be among your anchors for overcoming it.

And the next and the next and the next.

When I faced my cancer challenge from December 2012 through February 2013, on top of all the teaching I had received and Bible study I had performed on the subject, I also had years of believing God for small stuff like colds, sore throats, allergies, etc. under my belt. Whenever I face early cold symptoms, if I act immediately when my throat feels itchy and rebuke the attack in the name of Jesus, by God's grace it rarely develops into a full-blown cold.

So when I first heard the diagnosis of renal cell carcinoma, I already had experienced literally years of God demonstrating His willingness and ability to heal me. The idea He wouldn't honor His Word concerning that diagnosis was never a question in my mind because He had proven Himself faithful to His promises over time.

Someone can come along and try to argue with me how divine healing went away with the apostles (didn't he know that we still have apostles walking this planet even today? Doh!) or it's God's will for me to be sick so I can learn humility or some other such theological claptrap and I can look him square in the eye and say, "Too late! He's already healed me on multiple occasions, including cancer. I'll continue to believe the Word rather than your bogus religious traditions!"

Fair Warning: Don't Crater Your Future Blessings by Focussing on Your Past Ones

One of the fastest ways to shut down the flow of blessings from God in our lives is to start looking at His previous blessings and losing sight of Him. Doing so relegates those prior blessings to being one of the weights we are admonished to lay aside in Hebrews 12:1.

The Four Ps in Action

The classic example of the four Ps in action would be the children of Israel during their exodus from Egypt which we just discussed.

The Promise

There are 4 promises found in Exodus 3:18-22, so here's the list:

1. He will deliver them from Egyptian slavery.
2. He will bring them to a land flowing with milk and honey.
3. He will strike Egypt with supernatural judgements to induce Pharaoh's cooperation.
4. They will plunder the Egyptians before they leave Egypt.

The Principle

Trust God and obey Him.

The Problem

Pharaoh, the Egyptian army, the Sinai Wilderness, and the so-called giants in the Promised Land.

At the outset, the problem was Pharaoh himself, who oppressed the Israelites worse than ever once Moses approached him. Sometimes that happens to us, as well — the problem immediately gets worse, not better, and we wonder if we did the right thing.

But once Pharaoh relented and set them free, the Israelites did indeed plunder the Egyptians (how else did a bunch of slaves possess all that gold, precious jewels, and fancy cloth to construct and decorate that tent in the wilderness or cast that golden calf?).

Then, beginning with the Egyptian army at the Red Sea and ending with the evil report of the 10 spies sent into the Promised Land, the children of Israel faced a series of opportunities where they needed to respond in faith to God's promise. Instead, they responded with, "We were better off as slaves. You just brought us our here to die!" They were so consistent with that response that God finally threw up His hands and told them they would have what they had said. And so they spent the next 40 years in the wilderness until every one of that generation died off before the rest of them could enter into God's promise.

The Promise

Once the unbelieving generation had passed away, the next generation, led by Joshua, entered the Promised Land and, so long as they were obedient to whatever it was God had commanded of them, they won every battle and took the land.

Why Do Conditions Exist?

The problem with conditions is we have this innate ability to transform our compliance with them into dead religious works, thinking we have to earn stuff from God. But those conditions exist for a very different reason within God's plans and purposes for our lives, and I'm going to describe that reason now.

My Star Trek Revelation

As a fanatical science-fiction buff since childhood, I'm a big-time Trekkie, despite the entire Star Trek franchise being the ultimate expression of secular humanism, the antithesis of Christianity. While I missed out on the original series when it was first aired during my adolescence (my family had only one TV and my parents didn't care for sci-fi), I caught it in syndication as an adult and have watched every episode and movie since.

The second pilot in the original series, *"Where No Man Has Gone Before"*, debuts William Shatner as Captain Kirk and forms the backdrop for what I'm about to share. You are probably wondering how God can use a secular TV show, hang in there, I'm about to tell you!

Here are the broad strokes of the plot, courtesy of Wikipedia, because they summarized it ever so much better than I could have:

> *The starship USS Enterprise is on an exploratory mission to leave the galaxy. En route, a damaged ship's recorder of the SS Valiant, an Earth spaceship lost 200 years earlier, is found. Its record is incomplete, but it reveals that the Valiant had been swept from its path by a "magnetic space storm," and that the crew had frantically searched for information about extra-sensory perception (ESP) in the ship's library computer. The recording ends with the captain of the Valiant apparently giving a self-destruct order.*
>
> *Captain Kirk decides that they need to know what happened to the Valiant, and the Enterprise crosses the edge of the galaxy where it encounters a strange barrier which damages the ship's systems and warp drive, forcing a retreat. At the same time, nine crew members are killed and both helmsman Gary Mitchell and ship's psychiatrist Dr. Elizabeth Dehner are knocked unconscious by the barrier's effect. When he awakens, Mitchell's eyes glow silver, and he begins to display remarkable psychic powers.*
>
> *Mitchell becomes increasingly arrogant and hostile toward the rest of the crew, declaring that he has become godlike, enforcing his desires with fearsome displays of telepathic and telekinetic power. Science Officer Spock comes to believe that Valiant crew members may have experienced the same phenomenon, and destroyed the ship to keep the power from spreading. He advises Kirk that Mitchell may have to be killed before his powers develop further, but Kirk angrily disagrees.*

Alarmed that Mitchell may take over the Enterprise, Kirk decides to maroon him on an unmanned lithium-cracking facility on the remote planet of Delta Vega. Once there, the landing party tries to confine Mitchell, but his powers have become great. He goes on a rampage, kills navigator Lt. Lee Kelso and escapes, taking with him Dr. Dehner, who has now developed similar powers.

Kirk follows and appeals to Dr. Dehner's humanity for help. Before Mitchell can kill Kirk, the doctor attacks and weakens him. Mitchell fatally injures Dehner, but before he can recover from the effort, Kirk uses a phaser rifle to create a rock slide, killing Mitchell.

Two scenes in this episode are pertinent to my revelation:

1. After Mitchell escapes confinement and takes Dr. Dehner with him, he entices her to remain with him as "co-god" of that planet, showing her how they can provide for themselves by supernaturally creating a lush vegetable and fruit garden with a fresh-water spring on the barren rock planet surface.
2. In the episode's climax, Kirk heroically confronts Mitchell in order to save Dr. Dehner from him. In response, Mitchell declares himself to be God and forces Kirk to his knees with his hands together in an attitude of prayer, trying to coerce Kirk into praying to him and acknowledge his deity. Kirk resists, stammering out an appeal to Dr. Dehner's humanity, asking her if she sees "absolute power corrupting absolutely." Then Dr. Dehner indeed intervenes, and the story concludes as described in the plot summary above.

I was attending college on the GI Bill at the time to further develop my IT skills. Since my wife worked outside our home to support us while I was in school, I did quite a few of the household chores. While

I was vacuuming the living room after viewing this episode, the Lord wouldn't let me alone about what I had just seen.

What the Holy Spirit arrested my attention with was the juxtaposition of unlimited godhead power with Kirk's paraphrase of a political quote:

> *"Power corrupts, and absolute power corrupts absolutely"*
> *— Lord Acton (1834–1902)*

We've all heard this phrase whenever dealing with the likes of Hitler or Stalin. What the Holy Spirit arrested me with was coupling this phrase to *supernatural* — rather than political — power.

I then applied the verse in James saying, *"if any man lack wisdom, let him ask…"* and asked God what He was trying to tell me. He pointed me to the following New Testament passage:

> *Grace and peace be multiplied to you in the knowledge of God and of Jesus our Lord, as His divine power has given to us all things that pertain to life and godliness, through the knowledge of Him who called us by glory and virtue, by which have been given to us exceedingly great and precious promises, that through these you may be partakers of the divine nature, having escaped the corruption that is in the world through lust. — 2 Peter 1:2–4*

By that time in my ministry, I had taught this passage repeatedly, showing that, by believing the promises of God, we somehow became more like Him ("partakers of the divine nature").

I replied to the Lord, "Yes, I see this. You know I've been teaching from this passage for years."

He responded, *"What part of the promise imparts My nature to you?"*

When God asks a question, He is never seeking information because He already knows everything; I knew His query and its answer were the core of what God was trying to tell me. I thought about it for a bit, but couldn't come up with an answer, so I said, "I don't know, Lord."

His reply revolutionized my theology. He said, *"It's the condition! The more you fulfill the conditions of My promises, the more you are acting like Me. The more you act like Me, the more you actually become like Me because it becomes habit."*

It all suddenly fell into place as He reminded me of a quote I had once heard during a sermon on Christian character:

> *Sow a thought, reap a choice. Sow a choice, reap an action. Sow an action, reap a habit. Sow a habit, reap a character. Sow a character, reap a destiny. — Ralph Waldo Emerson*

Then the Lord pointed me to one of Jesus' parables:

> *For the kingdom of heaven is like a man traveling to a far country, who called his own servants and delivered his goods to them. And to one he gave five talents, to another two, and to another one, to each according to his own ability; and immediately he went on a journey.*
>
> *Then he who had received the five talents went and traded with them, and made another five talents and likewise he who had received two gained two more also, but he who had received one went and dug in the ground, and hid his lord's money.*
>
> *After a long time the lord of those servants came and settled accounts with them. So he who had received five talents came and brought five other talents, saying, 'Lord, you delivered to me five talents; look, I have gained five more talents besides them.' "His lord said to him, 'Well done, good and faithful servant;* ***you were faithful over a few things, I will make***

> ***you ruler over many things.*** *Enter into the joy of your lord.'…*
> *— Matthew 25:14–21 (emphasis mine)*

While there are several other things to be gleaned from this parable, the point I want to make here is the phrase boldfaced above. What the Lord showed me is this: *the more we are like Him, the more He can give us.*

Why?

Because whatever "it" is will not corrupt us as happened to Mitchell in the Star Trek episode. Then God gave me a more specific application:

> *Give, and it will be given to you: good measure, pressed down, shaken together, and running over will be put into your bosom. For with the same measure that you use, it will be measured back to you. — Luke 6:38*

What is an essential part of God's character? Loving generosity! When we give, we are imitating God, right? What happens when generous giving becomes a part of our lifestyle? It becomes part of our character. To the extent we are generous and unselfish with our substance, God can then entrust us with greater substance, knowing we will control it, rather than it controlling us!

That's why there are conditions for the promises governing our everyday relationships. Whenever we are conducting ourselves in agreement with the conditions in God's promises, those relationships exhibit the character of God as expressed in our love, generosity, forgiveness, righteousness, joy, and peace, just to name a few.

The conditions should never become a list of do's and don'ts, but things we do as children imitating our Heavenly Daddy. In the same manner that we reward our children for good behavior to develop their character, so too does God, and as we sow these things, we will indeed reap the harvest!

CHAPTER

13

Developing Your Faith

NOW THAT WE'VE ESTABLISHED WHAT faith is and how it works, let's discuss how to develop it. We've already covered in Chapter 9 how our faith is like a set of spiritual muscles. Those faith muscles grow stronger through opposition to adversity, just like our physical muscles do through opposing to gravity.

Just as you can use a training regimen of nutrition and exercise to increase your physical strength and endurance, you can also enter a spiritual regimen to bulk up your faith.

This chapter describes such a process.

What we will discuss here applies to any area of our lives, but for the sake of giving us something specific to hang these concepts on, we're going to apply them to physical healing.

Like Salvation, We Receive Healing by Faith

Receiving healing is just like receiving salvation: it's received by faith in God's Word, period.

We receive our salvation through a revelation of God's Word concerning His desire, willingness, and provision to save us from our sins through grace alone by our faith alone in the blood of Jesus Christ, the finished work of the cross, and His resurrection from the dead.

We receive that revelation through the enlightenment of the Holy Spirit, Who opens the Scriptures to us so that we can receive Christ. Part of that revelation includes the "how" of receiving salvation, that we are to confess Jesus as Lord and believe in our hearts God raised Him from the dead:

> *But what does it say? "The word is near you, in your mouth and in your heart" (that is, the word of faith which we preach): that if you confess with your mouth the Lord Jesus and believe in your heart that God has raised Him from the dead, you will be saved. For with the heart one believes unto righteousness, and with the mouth confession is made unto salvation. — Romans 10:9-10*

This is just the tip of the spiritual iceberg, however. We receive everything from God in precisely the same way: confessing with our mouths the Word of God and believing it in our hearts as we ask God to meet our needs in prayer.

Contemplate this tidbit for a moment: at the time we receive salvation, we typically know next to nothing about God and His incredible love for each of us. I mean, seriously! Think of what it is we actually are believing when we get saved:

> *Just over 2000 years ago, a Jewish carpenter of questionable parentage hiked around a small area of the Middle East preaching, performing amazing miracles, including raising the dead*

> *back to life while living a life totally devoid of selfishness. He proclaimed Himself to be God and the local officials of the day tortured and executed Him for that claim. But He really was and is God-in-Sandals and He arose from the dead 3 days after His execution. After His resurrection, He could walk through walls and travel around the countryside with no earthly means of transportation. The blood He shed washes away all the guilt and penalties for the past, present, and future selfish acts of all mankind. He gives us all of this as a free gift once we swear total allegiance to Him, allowing Him to run our lives as Absolute Ruler. Upon our own deaths, He allows us entrance into a place called Heaven where there are no tears, guilt, shame, or pain and we will live with Him there forever.*

No wonder Paul says in 1 Corinthians 1:23 this is foolishness to the Greeks (the humanist intellectuals of the era)! To the natural, unenlightened-by-the-Holy-Spirit human mind, what we believe is truly preposterous!

Yet Christ-followers do believe this essential truth to the point we are willing — and in certain areas of the modern world, still do! — suffer torture and even go to our own deaths singing praises to God rather than deny it (see Chapter 8). We also order our thinking and behaviors according to His precepts, rather than those espoused by the governments, cultures, and societies we live in. But I digress…

The primary issue preventing many believers from receiving divine healing is they do not accept and receive it by faith with the same tenacity and vigor they applied to their salvation.

How Much Faith is Enough?

Now some of you just read the previous paragraph and immediately assumed I am accusing people of not having enough faith. To which I would respond, "Well, how much is "'enough?'"

This "having enough faith" question puts the onus back on us and our performance, rather than focusing our attention where it should be: the grace of God and the Person and finished work of our loving Savior, Jesus Christ.

Once we shift our focus onto ourselves and our own performance, we immediately start thinking we need to do something to "prove" to God we have enough faith or are "worthy" to receive His blessings. This very mind-set drives the scripturally ignorant and spiritually immature to deny medical treatment for themselves and/or their children or make pilgrimages to "holy sites," such as the famous spring at Lourdes, France, or to attending evangelistic healing meeting after meeting, all the while trying to earn their healing from a God Who offers it as a free gift.

In other words, they operate on a healing-by-works basis, just as many try to operate on a salvation-by-works basis — neither gets them anywhere with God.

The encroachment of man's religion and God's view of it ("our righteousness is like filthy rags" — Isaiah 64:6) is in play in both cases. Interestingly, the Hebrew word for "filthy rags" in that verse literally translates as "a garment soiled from the waist down," which means our feeble and ineffective attempts to earn God's favor are about as valuable and useful as an infant's soiled diaper or a pair of skid-marked underwear!

Faith Comes By Revelation From God's Word

> *So then faith comes by hearing, and hearing by the word of God.*
> *— Romans 10:17*

hearing (*akoe*)

> *the sense of hearing; the organ of hearing, the ear; the thing heard*

word (*rhema*)

> *that which is or has been uttered by the living voice, thing spoken, word; any sound produced by the voice and having definite meaning; speech, discourse*

Faith results from our receiving heart-knowledge of God as revealed by the Holy Spirit through His spoken Word. If we have weak faith in some aspect of God's Word, it's because our revelation in that area is lacking or incorrect.

Returning to our previous illustration concerning salvation, when the Holy Spirit revealed to us how God provided the means for our salvation through Jesus, we responded in faith to that new knowledge, submitted our lives to the Lordship of Jesus, and received the New Birth. When the Holy Spirit reveals God has also provided the means for our healing through Jesus, we respond in faith and get healed.

The issue here is not one of us having "enough faith," but is our level of revelation sufficient for the task at hand? Which leads us to a fundamental truism of Christianity:

> *All our "faith problems" result from an insufficient or inaccurate revelation of God's character, will, and/or ability.*

Let's break this down in a bit more detail.

God's Will

As we have already discussed in Chapter 7, God's will is His Word. If He promises something in the Bible and we are operating in all the conditions — if any — attached to that promise, He will affirmatively answer a prayer based upon that promise every time, without exception. There may be a time lag between the provision and the prayer. He may answer by a different means than we have preconceived with our puny human intellects, but God is faithful — He will deliver what He has promised.

God's Character, Part 1

God is good, and He does not visit evil upon His children. That being said, He can and does allow us to experience the consequences of our bad choices. He will also withhold earthly blessings whenever we are willfully disobedient.

If a human father were to harm his children physically or infect them with a sickness to teach them a lesson in humility, obedience, or whatever, it would horrify us. Such behavior should justly put that demented father in jail for child abuse. Yet, somehow, Catholics and Calvinists believe that our Heavenly Father does precisely those sorts of things for precisely the same purposes. Their escape clause is God has thoughts higher than our thoughts and His plan will somehow come out for our good, even though we cannot see it.

However, nowhere do we see this demonstrated in the life and ministry of Jesus Christ during His earthly ministry. Indeed, Jesus Himself touched on this issue in His Sermon on the Mount:

> *If you then, being evil, know how to give good gifts to your children, how much more will your Father Who is in heaven give good things to those who ask Him! — Matthew 7:11*

God's Character, Part 2

The Scriptures repeat over and over how God is not a respecter of persons. This means He is totally impartial in dispensing both blessings and justice.

Considering what we have discussed earlier about our total unworthiness to receive anything from God apart from His grace, there are no "superstars" in the Body of Christ. As my favorite Billy Graham quote states, "the ground is always level at the foot of the Cross," so there is no "high ground" — moral or otherwise — for any human to stake out, claiming special access to or favor with God.

The bottom line is this: if God will answer the prayers of Billy Graham or some other mighty man or woman of God we admire, He will answer yours, too!

God's Ability

God is omnipotent, the $10 theological term meaning "all-powerful, infinitely capable, possessing limitless ability." Whenever we speak His Word, it carries the same creative and miraculous power it did when He originally spoke them.

The selfsame God who spun the universe into existence and keeps it running by His Word also possesses all the power, energy, means, whatever required for Him to deliver on any promise He has made to us. Whether He heals us by supernatural miraculous means or through human medicine, it's all the same to Him.

Examples

- If I have never even heard of the concept of God's provision for salvation or healing in the Scriptures, I have an *insufficient revelation* of God's Word, so I will have faith for neither. Therefore, I will remain unsaved and/or unhealed.
- If I have the erroneous impression I can earn God's favor and get salvation/healing/whatever from Him through my dead religious works, I have an *incorrect revelation* of His Word regarding God's abundant grace. Because of this, I cannot see how everything I receive from Him is a gift offered through His boundless love, despite my perpetual inability to meet His standards of perfection in thought and behavior.
- If I think any of the problems I face are beyond God's ability to overcome, I have an *insufficient revelation* of His unlimited ability.
- If I believe God will answer the prayers of my pastor or other person whom I admire and respect as a "holy man," but not

my own, I have an *incorrect revelation* of God's character. The One True God is not a respecter of persons and answers every believer's prayers.

- And so on...

How We Receive Revelation

Two passages contain the primary principles in play here:

Passage #1

> *And do not be conformed to this world, but be transformed by the renewing of your mind, that you may prove what is that good and acceptable and perfect will of God. — Romans 12:2*

Let's unpack this verse:

conformed (***suschematizo***)

> *to conform one's self (i.e. one's mind and character) to another's pattern, (fashion one's self according to) NOTE: It carries the connotation of being squeezed into a mold by pressure.*

world (***aion***)

> *This is where we get the word "eon" to denote a period of time. In this verse, it carries the connotation of "the culture and mores of this age."*

transformed (***metamorphoo***)

> *to change into another form, to transform, to transfigure.*

Metamorphoo is the same term used in the Gospel accounts of the Mount of Transfiguration when it says that Jesus was "transfigured." It's also the Greek word where we derive the English terms "metamorphosis" and "metamorphic."

The dictionary defines "metamorphosis" as "a change of the form or nature of a thing or person into a completely different one, by natural or supernatural means." Thus,

- A hideous caterpillar spins a cocoon around itself and transforms itself into a gorgeous butterfly through metamorphosis.
- By metamorphosis, an ugly lump of soft coal, by a combination of heat and pressure, is transformed into the hardest rock in the world as well as one of the most stunningly beautiful and valuable, a diamond.

renewing (*anakainosis*)

> *a renewal, renovation, complete change for the better"*

prove (*dokimazo*)

> *to test, examine, prove, scrutinise (to see whether or not a thing is genuine), as metals; to recognize as genuine after examination, to approve, deem worthy*

A more in-depth translation would read like this:

> *Do not be conformed to this world (this age), [fashioned after and adapted to its external, superficial customs], but be transformed (changed) by the [entire] renewal of your mind [by its new ideals and its new attitude], so that you may prove [for yourselves] what is the good and acceptable and perfect will of God, even the thing which is good and acceptable and perfect [in His sight for you]. — Romans 12:2 AMP*

If I want to test and see what the good, true, and perfect will of God is, I must allow God to renew my mind, so I am transformed from someone who does not believe some aspect of His Word into someone who not only grasps it intellectually, but has tested and proven it by experience.

Passage #2

> *Grace and peace be multiplied to you in the knowledge of God and of Jesus our Lord, as His divine power has given to us all things that pertain to life and godliness, through the knowledge of Him who called us by glory and virtue, by which have been given to us exceedingly great and precious promises, that through these you may be partakers of the divine nature, having escaped the corruption that is in the world through lust. — 2 Peter 1:2–4*

Here, we first see how grace and peace are multiplied — not added — to us through our knowledge of God. We further discover how all things pertaining to "life and godliness" come through that self-same knowledge.

Unfortunately, the vast majority of us blow past the phrase "knowledge of God," unconsciously retranslating it in our minds to "knowledge about God."

The difference here is crucial!

The Holy Spirit speaking through Peter here is declaring how grace, peace, our personal godliness, and everything else pertaining to our lives in general come through knowing God, not knowing information about Him.

The original Greek bears this out. The word for "knowledge" used in both places is the word *epignosis*, whose literal translation is "precise and correct knowledge." But there is a connotation to this word carrying an even deeper meaning: *such knowledge is experiential in nature.* This means we know God with a certitude based upon our relationship with Him, as opposed to our intellectual acceptance of theological principles read in a book or taught from a pulpit.

Through our accurately and experientially knowing God, He has given us His "great and precious promises" so we "may be partakers of the divine nature, having escaped the corruption which is in the world through lust." Let's delve into that last phrase further:

partakers (kiononos)

a partner, associate, comrade, companion in something.

corruption (*phthora*)

corruption, destruction, perishing"

lust (*epithumia*)

desire, craving, longing, desire for what is forbidden, lust

This phrase literally means we can become partners, associates and companions in the very character of God and escape the destruction and perishing in this world, a world filled with — and ruled by — selfish desires (aka sin).

Since we know there was no evil — including sickness — in the Garden of Eden, we can also safely conclude disease entered this world through Adam's and Eve's desire for what was forbidden. We know sickness and diseases corrupt and destroy our bodies. So, even though divine healing is not specifically called out in this passage, its inclusion is implied.

Putting These Principles Into Practice

The bottom line of all this is *mind renewal.* This means we do not allow ourselves to be squeezed into the thinking patterns of this world system or religious traditions penned by long-dead theologians, but allow our minds to be changed in conformity to the good and true and perfect will of God for us, His Word.

Such experiential and accurate knowledge will enable us to escape not only sin, but sickness and disease through God's precious promises, also found in His Word.

I'm going to present this process as a list, specifically targeting healing, though you can apply these principles to any other matter for which you desire to discover God's will and develop faith in it.

Danger! Danger, Will Robinson!

The inherent hazard to my presenting all this in list form is you might take it as a recipe or formula of dead religious works necessary to please God.

I intend nothing of the sort! Indeed, my goal is precisely the opposite.

I am not describing a recipe, but an exercise in positioning yourself to allow God to reveal Himself to you in a deeper way concerning divine healing.

God wants your thinking to be transformed to agree with His, a position of incredible spiritual strength. Through that process, you come to know Jesus more fully and accurately. From there, you can avail yourself of God's promises and receive your healing.

#1: Seek God: Foremost, pray and ask the same Holy Spirit Who authored the Bible to reveal whatever Truth He feels is necessary for you to have a working revelation of God's character, will, and ability concerning healing.

#2: Study God's Word: Use whatever study aids you have available (a physical concordance, computer-based Bible study app or a reputable website such Bible.com) to perform word searches on various terms related to healing (e.g., healing, healed, made whole, delivered, etc.) in both the Old and New Testaments.

After assembling your lists of verses, read each of them in their context.

#3: Confess Aloud: Read these verses aloud to yourself. Some have scoffed at the "aloud" portion of this, questioning its value and validity, or have dismissed it as cultish mind science. Mind science is indeed a satanic counterfeit — it is also a fundamental truism there must be an authentic version of something somewhere for a counterfeit to be made of it. *This is the true original.*

Scientific studies have proven that whenever we speak, we have no choice but to believe what we say. We can — and often do — filter out what other people say verbally and in print because of our own preconceptions, assumptions, prejudices, and emotional strongholds, but whenever we speak to ourselves aloud, we bypass those filters and our subconscious minds accept without question whatever it is we've said.

Whenever we speak aloud thoughts/ideas contrary to the Word of God, that's what we will accept as true. We will then think and act accordingly. However, if we speak aloud God's Word, that's what we will believe to be true — our attitudes, beliefs, and behaviors will follow.

This is why healthy self-talk (what we say to ourselves about ourselves) is so crucial. If we repeat to ourselves the jackal voices of our childhoods (you're nothing, you're a failure, you're a loser, you're stupid, etc.), we will continue to behave in precisely those patterns.

There is a significant benefit to putting God's promises into the first person when doing this. Replace any pronouns in the verse with "I," "me," and so on, then adjust the remaining grammar accordingly. For example, instead of reading Isaiah 53:5 aloud as originally written:

> *But He was wounded for our transgressions, He was bruised for our iniquities; the chastisement for our peace was upon Him, and by His stripes we are healed.*

Read it instead as:

> *But He was wounded for my transgressions, He was bruised for my iniquities; the chastisement for my peace was upon Him, and by His stripes I am healed.*

#4: Receive Revelation & Pray: As you are doing Steps #1-3, the Holy Spirit will make one or more passages you are reading come alive aka "jump out at you." Whenever that occurs, that's a verse He wants you to stand in faith upon. Pray and ask God for your healing based upon that scripture verse/passage, thanking Him for your healing as an accomplished fact. For example, if God quickens Isaiah 53:4-5 to you, then you can pray:

> *"Lord, I believe that Jesus has borne my sicknesses and carried my pains, and by His stripes I was healed, so based upon your Word, I ask You to heal my _________."*

#5: Offer Thanks: After your initial prayer, regularly and — especially if your symptoms continue or escalate — thank God for healing your body based upon the verse you initially prayed. If the doctors give you bad news concerning your situation, say something like "I'm not moved by what I see or hear, but by the Word of God which says…" and quote that verse again.

Continue to thank God for His healing you. Apart from the obvious reasons of why we should be grateful to God for anything and everything, why is this important? Here's why: maintaining an attitude of thankfulness helps keep your faith on track.

If you, as a rational person, are going to thank someone for future delivery on a promise given you today, you must be convinced the person who made it has the character and ability to deliver the goods. Just today, a friend offered to give me a nice computer he had lying around gathering dust. I thanked him for it immediately because I can trust him to be a man of his word.

So by thanking God, we are putting ourselves into the mind-set His promise is true and we will indeed receive whatever He has promised.

We should never see or use thankfulness as an expression of entitlement before God. Everything He promises is by His limitless grace, but He will not allow Himself to be treated like some sort of cosmic bellhop or servant of a mere human. We work for Him, not the other way around!

#6: Faith Becomes Heart Knowledge: Somewhere along the way, you are going to experience your verse as "heart knowledge." This means you have become fully persuaded in your belief the verse God has shown you is indeed the Truth, the whole Truth, and nothing but the Truth.

When this happens concerning the New Birth, we call it "assurance of salvation" which means we no longer have any doubts we are indeed saved and going to heaven — we just know in our "knower" and no one and nothing thereafter can talk us out of that conviction.

Receiving heart knowledge that you are healed based upon the verse(s) God has revealed to you is no different. Thereafter, you will respond instantly in your faith in God's Word regarding healing to all attacks of sickness upon your body.

#7: Avoid Denial: As we've already discussed in the previous chapter, denial is our refusing to deal with reality, saying, "I'm not sick, I'm not sick, I'm not sick!" whereas genuine faith is our proclamation of the superior, spiritual reality, saying, "By His stripes I'm healed!"

#8: Obey God: If God tells you to do something specific, obey Him, period!

- If He tells you to forgive someone, stop making excuses and do it!
- If He tells you to restore a broken relationship, stop making excuses and do it!
- If you are doing something detrimental for your health and He tells you to stop, stop making excuses and do it!

His grace is more than enough to empower you to obey Him, but don't expect God to answer your prayers while living a self-directed life.

#9: Persevere: Continue doing these things until either:

1. The symptoms go away, and/or;
2. The doctors confirm your healing and you require no further treatment.

Conclusion

So that's how it's done. The principles are the same, no matter what you are believing God for.

AUTHOR'S NOTE: I have presented throughout my writings it is always God's will to heal us at all times and in all places. That being said, nowhere have I ever advocated or even hinted you should refuse medical treatment or to follow sound medical advice!

God uses medicine and medical professionals regularly to bring healing to our bodies. I am a living testimony to the fact that Jehovah-Rapha uses both supernatural and medical science to heal our physical bodies.

Through God's general grace, medical professionals serve a divine calling placed within them at birth by their Creator. Good ones are operating under His healing anointing, even though they may not be Christ-followers or even acknowledge He exists.

Refusing medical treatment is a sign of spiritual ignorance and/or immaturity — *how* God heals us is *His* choice, *never ours.*

CHAPTER

14

Talking to Mountains?

WHEN I TAUGHT ON PRAYER at a Bible study several years ago, I stated there are models taught in the Bible on how to pray. One of those present quickly challenged my statement, demanding: "You mean we have to pray a certain way or we won't get our prayers answered!?"

To which I replied, "No, because that would be a legalistic recipe for dead religious works — the very essence of man's religion — and our God doesn't operate that way."

That being said, however, Jesus Himself taught principles and precepts which can greatly enhance our prayer lives — ignoring them serves us poorly.

What I'm about to share is straight from the mouth of Jesus, so any quibble you have with what I am about to teach is with Him, not me!

Jesus vs. the Fig Tree

Fascinatingly, there are only two recorded instances where Jesus directly taught his disciples on how to pray. One of them, the Lord's Prayer, receives almost all the attention from pulpits. Given the minimal amount of air-time given the second one, you'd think it doesn't even exist in Scripture.

In this chapter, we're going to be examining the second one, which is found in Mark 11:20-26.

To establish context, a few verses prior, Jesus attempted to pick some fruit from a nearby fig tree as He passed it on the way into Jerusalem. He found the tree barren. His response was to curse it (the passage specifically notes how the disciples heard Him say this), after which He entered the city and cleansed the temple.

We'll take up the narrative in the verse where they exited Jerusalem the very next day and discovered the selfsame tree had withered from the roots overnight:

> *Now in the morning, as they passed by, they saw the fig tree dried up from the roots. And Peter, remembering, said to Him, 'Rabbi, look! The fig tree which You cursed has withered away.'*
>
> *So Jesus answered and said to them, 'Have faith in God. For assuredly, I say to you, whoever says to this mountain, "Be removed and be cast into the sea," and does not doubt in his heart, but believes that those things he says will be done, he will have whatever he says.*
>
> *Therefore, I say to you, whatever things you ask when you pray, believe that you receive them, and you will have them. And whenever you stand praying, if you have anything against anyone, forgive him, that your Father in heaven may also forgive*

> *you your trespasses. But if you do not forgive, neither will your Father in heaven forgive your trespasses.' — Mark 11:20-26*

Let's unpack this concept by concept:

#1: Have Faith in God: We've just spent two lengthy chapters describing both how faith works and how to develop it, so I will simply use this opportunity to reinforce the idea Jesus put faith at the top of the list. None of the rest of this list works apart from faith in God's Word.

#2: Command the Mountain: Then Jesus said we should speak to mountains. This, on its surface, sounds ludicrous and is something of a mind-bender. I mean, how many of us have walked over to the nearest hill and started talking to it? But if God-in-Sandals says we should talk to mountains, who are we to argue?

One time, my pastor in Wichita was preaching on this passage and proclaimed we could develop enough faith to "move all the mountains in Kansas." I inquired of him after the service, "But Pastor Rob, if we moved every mountain in Kansas, wouldn't all the freeway overpasses collapse?" (if you've never been to Kansas, you won't get that joke!).

All kidding aside, though, Jesus was speaking of figurative mountains here, though I expect He personally could have pulled off moving an actual mountain because — unlike us! — He had perfect trust in our Heavenly Father and no corrupt flesh nature to hinder either his faith or his authority — His speaking to that fig tree certainly proved effective!

We all have mountains in our lives. What are they?

Negative circumstances!

We face mountains of:

- Sickness
- Financial lack

- Relational problems within our families
- Unemployment or employment difficulties
- Addiction
- Depression
- Bitterness towards those who have abused or neglected us
- The list goes on and on…

And what are we supposed to be doing about those mountains? Speaking to them — more specifically *commanding* them — to be removed from our lives.

This kind of mountain moving is well within our wheelhouse as Christ-followers. Our trouble with this concept is getting past that initial feeling of silliness Satan uses to discourage/dissuade us from doing so. He wants to keep us from removing those mountains he so evilly and intentionally put in our lives to discourage and/or destroy us. Once we're past the initial hurdle of self-consciousness, speaking to our mountains becomes more and more second-nature as we practice it.

In Chapter 6, we discussed our God-given authority as believers. Commanding mountains is how we express that authority on this earth. When we have financial lack, we take authority over that "mountain" and speak to it, saying something like, "I command financial lack to loose us and depart in the name of Jesus. Thank you, Lord, that all our bills are paid current and we have more than enough to be generous."

Or when faced with symptoms of illness, we can say something like, "I curse these symptoms along with whatever germs are causing them. I command them to wither and die and loose my body and depart in Jesus' name!"

Or when coming out under the bondage of an addiction, "Heavenly Father, I thank you the blood of Jesus and the finished work of the cross have completely delivered me from all addictions and compulsive behaviors. I curse this addiction and command it to wither and die. I declare myself free in Jesus' name!"

#3: Praying in Faith, Receiving: This is yet another principle most Christians totally miss: receiving! Most of us "ask" when we pray, but never "receive" the answer before it actually manifests.

When Jesus speaks of "receiving" here in this passage, He's not talking about the actual answer coming down the road. He said, *"When you pray, receive…"*

So how do you receive something? The best example is when someone gives us a gift. When they hand it to us, we accept it into our possession and thereafter own it. That is "receiving."

Jesus is telling us we are to accept into our personal ownership whatever it is we are praying for *at the time we are praying for it!*

The psychological implication is this: if we have received ownership of whatever we have prayed for, it precludes any idea God will not answer our prayer affirmatively.

And who wants to take what is ours? Satan, who steals, kills, and destroys (John 10:10). How does he steal it? By convincing us with his lies that God will not answer our prayers because of some reason or another, or to get us to back off from doing what God has commanded us to do.

In summary, he can only steal what he can talk us out of! As we've already covered, we are fighting a defensive battle to protect what is already ours, not fighting an offensive battle to obtain it.

#4: Forgiving: I'll explore this subject in great depth in the following chapter because of its monumental impact on the topic at hand. Unforgiveness is a huge sticking point with God, so whatever you may harbor against whoever "done you dirt," give it up, give it to God, and forgive!

The Principle of Binding & Loosing

In my example prayers a couple of pages ago, you may have noticed I mentioned "loosing" ourselves from negative circumstances. This concept and practice comes from the following verse in the Gospel of Matthew, where again Jesus is speaking:

> *Assuredly, I say to you, whatever you bind on earth will be bound in heaven, and whatever you loose on earth will be loosed in heaven. — Matthew 18:18*

This is yet another manifestation of Jesus' restoration of our authority over this earth. Let's look at these words in the Greek:

bind (*deo*)

> *to bind, tie, or fasten*

loose (*luo*)

> *to untie someone who is bound, to set free, to discharge from prison*

Here's how this works in prayer: we loose ourselves or whoever else we are praying for, from whatever bondage or difficulty we or they are in. Then we bind ourselves or them to the plans, purposes, destiny of God, as well as His applicable promises.

Putting It All Together

Taking these principles altogether, let's look at a couple of sample prayers, first for healing:

> *Heavenly Father, Your Word says that Jesus bore my sicknesses and carried my pains and by His stripes I am healed. You*

also have declared in Your Word that You are Jehovah-Rapha, the God Who heals us. Regardless of how I feel or the doctors' diagnosis, I believe your Word. I speak to this mountain of ___________ (fill in the diagnosis) and command it to loose my body and depart in Jesus' name and in that same name I bind myself to the healing power of God. I receive complete restoration of my physical health in the wonderful name of Jesus.

Here's a second example, this time for financial provision, paraphrasing Philippians 4:19 as well as 2 Corinthians 9:8 from the Amplified Version:

"Heavenly Father, I thank You that You are Jehovah-Jireh, the God Who sees in advance and provides. Your Word says that all my needs are met according to your riches in glory in Christ Jesus and You have made every favor and earthly blessing come to me in abundance, so that I always and under all circumstances and whatever the need, possess enough to require no aid or support. I am furnished in abundance for every good work and charitable donation.

I choose to believe your promises despite what I see with my eyes and what the circumstances tell me. I speak to this mountain of financial lack in the name of Jesus and command it to be uprooted and cast into the sea. Be obliterated from my life!. I command my bank account to be full and I receive your financial provision into my life. I loose myself from poverty and lack and bind myself to Your divine provision for my life in Jesus' mighty name."

Now I just wrote those out of personal experience, roughly how I've prayed about those same issues in times past.

These are neither recipes nor are they incantations — *they are examples.*

Use them until you can riff such a prayer from your own heart — there is nothing special about these words in and of themselves.

As we discussed in this chapter, as well as the two previous ones, no matter whose words you use, *you must believe them!*

Faith is how it all works and, as I've already covered earlier, developing your faith is a growth process. You start out small, taking baby steps, and allow God to show Himself mighty on your behalf in minor issues. As you grow, the challenges will grow with you.

In conclusion, let me reiterate, there is no one on the sidelines holding up score cards for technical excellence and artistic expression when you pray — other than the devil himself. And it is he who will lie his face off trying to talk you out of everything I've been teaching here.

Don't let him!

CHAPTER

15

The Crucial Process of Forgiveness

IN THE PREVIOUS CHAPTER, I MENTIONED the centrality of forgiving others to a successful prayer life and promised we would explore forgiveness in far greater depth in this one.

Here we go!

In 2012, my high school class from San Leandro High School in San Leandro, California celebrated its 40th reunion. I had planned to show up when first I heard about it until the Lord convicted me I was going to attend with the wrong motives. Since God is far more concerned about the motivations of our hearts than outward appearances, I needed to repent and get things right.

So in obedience to Him, I stayed home and instead bore witness to the cause of Christ and His miraculous doings in my life during the 39 years since I had seen them last.

What follows is the post, with only minor edits, I wrote to the Facebook group created for that reunion explaining my absence from the event. It also contains quite a bit of my early personal history few people know about, not even my brothers and sisters in Christ. After reading that, we'll delve into forgiveness in depth and discover out why it is so important.

The Facebook Post

> *"God has been dealing with me about my motives for attending the reunion this summer. My conclusion is that it would be inappropriate for my wife and me to attend.*
>
> *"My reasons? Almost none of you know my story and it will help you understand my decision once you do.*
>
> *"Before I showed up in San Leandro, I was a native resident of El Paso, Texas. At school there, I suffered a great deal of abuse at the hands of various teachers and administrators, abuse that, were it to have taken place today, would have seen the perpetrators summarily fired as well as publicly castigated and humiliated in the press.*
>
> *"The abuse stemmed from the teachers and administrators at school being completely unable to cope with the perfect storm of my above-average intelligence, my undiagnosed-until-2nd-grade nearsightedness coupled with a last name constantly placing me at the back of the classroom, my undiagnosed-until-age-40 Attention Deficit Disorder (ADD), and my complete lack of any vestige of athletic prowess. In modern terms, I was the archetypical nerd with a short attention span!*
>
> *"My schoolmates saw the way those officials treated me and determined I was fair game for their own rejection and bullying. By the time I had endured 8 years of this during kindergarten through 7th grade, I was neurotic and emotionally needy to the point that, when I arrived in California after my*

father's near-fatal heart attack, I brought all those problems with me. The vast majority of you simply took up where my former tormentors in Texas had left off.

"The Wizard of Oz was my favorite movie throughout childhood and I still tear up whenever I hear Over The Rainbow. *I recently heard the song playing over the Muzak system at the local mall and tried to explain to my wife its emotional impact on me. As I did so, I suddenly realized that it echoed the emotions of a desperately lonely boy who desperately wanted to be ANYone else, ANYwhere else than who and where he was.*

"So I endured, rather than enjoyed, my time at Bancroft Junior High and SLHS and, truth be told, I cannot recall much of it I care to celebrate. Glenn {last name omitted} and Bob {last name omitted}, fellow outcasts, were my only friends at SLHS. We treasure our friendship to this day.

"Amazingly enough, I discovered others during my SLHS years who I, in turn, could look down upon to make me feel better about myself: Tony {last name omitted} and Robert {last name omitted}, to name two.

"It was only by the grace of God during our senior year I didn't end up in juvenile prison or worse from an occasion when one member of this very Facebook group accosted me in the hallway one day, threatening me with a serious beating over a prior incident where his girlfriend ran my bicycle off the road with her car and then physically assaulted me — I had pepper-sprayed her to avoid hitting her back.

"What he didn't know at the time was that I had a 5-inch razor-honed switchblade knife in my jacket pocket (it was my constant companion every school day, I might add). It was in my hand with my thumb on the button as he cornered me with

his forearm across my throat, his face only a few inches from mine. Though completely terrified, I was equally determined to do my best to kill him rather than submit to that indignity. Fortunately for us both, he relented — had he delivered that first blow, he never would have seen the blade coming and both of our lives would have changed drastically for the worse in ways I cannot even imagine.

"Another time, prior to my acquiring the knife, I had to break a 2-quart Coke bottle on the curb to arm myself against two other bullies who were following me home with evil intentions. When they saw I was ready to shed their blood to defend myself, their agenda immediately changed, and they backed off.

"Those were just three moments in the social hell I lived in during junior high and high school, but they define that time well.

"Three months after graduation, I enlisted in the Army. After training, they stationed me in Germany, where I met Jesus. While I had attended various Lutheran churches my entire life up to that point, I had never had a personal relationship with Him until I ran 6,000+ miles from everyone and everything I had ever known, straight into His loving arms.

"Jesus rescued me from the self-hatred, rejection, and emotional neediness which had dominated my early life. Had He not intervened in my life, I quite possibly would have ended up either as a serial killer or a suicide because of the incredible rage and pain I carried within me.

Yet another act of His grace, to my eternal gratitude towards Him, is it never even crossed my mind to stage my own personal Columbine massacre there at SLHS — I certainly had the rage, the poor self-image, the expert skill as a pistol shooter, and the access to firearms required to put such a plan into action.

"Jesus transformed my life. He took an angry, scared, rebellious, insecure boy and over the years between then and now:

- *"Showed me what it was to be loved and accepted apart from my performance or lack thereof.*

- *"He called me into His ministry and gifted me with the abilities to teach and preach His Word as well as counsel the abused and addicted.*

- *"He gave me a wonderful, lovely, godly wife, calling her to my side from halfway around the world and, against all odds, somehow influenced her to love me — outside of my salvation, she is God's greatest gift to me.*

- *"He has given me a career as an IT professional, graphic artist, and website designer that has earned me the respect of my friends, associates, and professional peers.*

- *"He has gifted me with two awesome children, one by birth, the other by adoption, who are absolute joys.*

- *"And despite my many, many stupid choices over the years, he has continued to love me, guide me, correct me, encourage me, heal me, anoint me, and—most importantly — deliver me from impulsively running off my mouth and hurting people.*

"The famous missionary Dr. David Livingston of "Dr.-Livingston-I-presume" fame said it perfectly:

> *All that I am I owe to Jesus Christ, revealed to me in His divine book.*

"I've said all that to say this: my attitude when I first RSVPed was I would show up with kind of an "in-your-face" attitude, accompanied by my beautiful wife and armed with a list of career

successes as proving the lot of you had totally misjudged me, that I have significance as a person, and I indeed have something of value to offer to others.

"What the Lord has shown me is doing so would be like being born on third base and claiming I hit a triple. I cannot lay claim to being or doing anything of earthly or heavenly value He has not produced in my life by the power of His Word and His limitless grace. So I'm going to continue to let Him do some more healing on me, renewing my heart and mind on an even deeper level than before.

"He also revealed that I needed to walk in a greater level of forgiveness towards you, though I had already started that process quite a while back. Christ set the example for me with some of His last words from the cross:

> *Father, forgive them, for they know not what they do.*
>
> *— Luke 23:34*

"Regardless of your attitude towards me, then or now, I have only one thing to say:

"I FORGIVE YOU.

"I'm praying everyone of you comes to know the same divine love and forgiveness I have experienced for almost 39 years. I pray that, in knowing Him, you spend the rest of your lives experiencing His awesome "peace that surpasses all understanding."

"And if any of you ever run across Tony or Robert, I owe them an apology. Please let me know how I can reach them.

Why I Included This Story

Some of you may ask yourselves why this story appears here. After all, some of it is pretty personal and revealing.

My answer is this: I'm but one of a gazillion people on this planet who have been abused and bullied by their teachers, school administrators, and classmates, not to mention family members. I am showing, through my own life, how to engage in overcoming such abuse through forgiveness.

To wrap that incident up, here's how everyone reacted. I had expected, even after 40 years, the universal rejection would continue as before. However — and much to my surprise! — many of those who had rejected me back in the day were openly and sincerely shocked at my story and grieved I had suffered so. One of them, an educator, was so moved she added bullying to the agenda for a meeting she was chairing. Of course, the believers among them immediately "got it" and several of them are friends now.

The rest? Well, let's just say their insensitivity and callousness have not abated over the years. The jock who cornered me in the hallway that day didn't care enough to apologize, so he stayed true to form as well.

But the freedom I've experienced since obeying God in this area has been wonderful, so how anyone else coulda/shoulda/kinda/definitely reacted is entirely irrelevant. They are responsible before God for their behavior and Isaiah 54:17 is very much the operative Scripture for them.

Why is Forgiveness so Important?

One thing Jesus spent more than a few verses addressing in the Gospels is the concept of forgiveness. The apostles also dealt with that topic in virtually every letter they wrote. Of them all, our keynote passage for this chapter will be:

> *Pursue peace with all people, and holiness, without which no one will see the Lord: looking carefully lest anyone fall short of the grace of God; lest any root of bitterness springing up cause trouble, and by this many become defiled. — Hebrews 12:14-15*

> *Forgiveness doesn't excuse their behavior. Forgiveness prevents their behavior from destroying your heart.*

I've said it before and I'll say it again here: we never sin in a vacuum! Who knows the so-called "secret" sins we commit with no one else on earth knowing about them? Everyone inhabiting the spirit realm: God and His angels, and Satan and his demons! Our selfish acts ripple away from us and corrupt every one of our relationships with other people on some level or another, especially our families. The verse in Exodus where it speaks of the sins of the fathers being visited on the 3rd and 4th generations is in play here.

The top of that secret sin list for the vast majority of humanity is idolatry, followed closely by the second one: unforgiveness. Not lust, not greed, not gluttony, but a refusal to forgive.

When we allow unforgiveness to take root and turn us bitter, it can and does drive all kinds of compulsive behaviors and addictions, especially rage-aholism.

That's why one of the crucial steps in any 12-step addiction recovery program (all the steps are based in the Scriptures, I might add) is to forgive all those who have wronged us, no matter how heinous those sins against us may have been. There's a saying in recovery circles which perfectly illustrates the point I'm making here:

Refusing to forgive is like you taking poison and expecting the other person to die.

Unforgiveness is toxic, so toxic that bitterness has been linked to cancer and heart disease in people's physical bodies. Like cancer does in a body, bitterness eats away at our souls, taking over healthy areas until our whole mental and emotional being is affected.

Eventually, we die of it.

The Parable of the Two Servants

Our refusing to forgive is also a manifestation of self-lordship, an area where we insist on being on the throne of our lives ourselves instead of Jesus.

That, of course, is *never* a safe place to be!

Jesus specifically addresses this issue in one of my favorite parables:

Then Peter came to Him and said, "Lord, how often shall my brother sin against me, and I forgive him? Up to seven times?" Jesus said to him, "I do not say to you, up to seven times, but up to seventy times seven.

"Therefore the kingdom of heaven is like a certain king who wanted to settle accounts with his servants. And when he had begun to settle accounts, one was brought to him who owed him 10,000 talents. But as he was not able to pay, his master commanded that he be sold, with his wife and children and all that he had, and that payment be made.

> *"The servant therefore fell down before him, saying, 'Master, have patience with me, and I will pay you all.' Then the master of that servant was moved with compassion, released him, and forgave him the debt.*
>
> *"But that servant went out and found one of his fellow servants who owed him 100 denarii; and he laid hands on him and took him by the throat, saying, 'Pay me what you owe!'*
>
> *"So his fellow servant fell down at his feet and begged him, saying, 'Have patience with me, and I will pay you all.'*
>
> *And he would not, but went and threw him into prison till he should pay the debt. So when his fellow servants saw what had been done, they were very grieved, and came and told their master all that had been done.*
>
> *"Then his master, after he had called him, said to him, 'You wicked servant! I forgave you all that debt because you begged me. 'Should you not also have had compassion on your fellow servant, just as I had pity on you?' And his master was angry, and delivered him to the torturers until he should pay all that was due to him.*
>
> *"So My heavenly Father also will do to you if each of you, from his heart, does not forgive his brother his trespasses."*
>
> — *Matthew 18:21-35*

Let's unpack this story.

The First Servant

First, what is a "talent?" The Bible is not referring to innate human skills and natural abilities, but to an ancient unit of currency.

There were two kinds of talents in Jesus' day, one silver, the other gold.

- A silver talent was roughly 100 pounds of silver.
- A gold talent was about twice that weight in gold.

As of this writing, gold is being traded at about $1900/ounce and silver for about $30/ounce. We don't know whether the talents in this parable were silver or gold ones, so we can only guesstimate the amount the first servant owned was between close to $42,000 (silver) or just over $6,000,000 (gold) in US dollars.

We have no way of ascertaining the relative values of silver and gold to one another in biblical times because such records simply do not exist. I personally believe Jesus was referring to gold talents.

Why do I say this?

Because I believe He was trying to make a point to His listeners: the amount owed by the first servant was a stratospheric sum beyond Peter's and the others' abilities to imagine owning or owing.

Since this is strictly my opinion, you are under no obligation to agree with me, but since it's my book, I'll continue with our analysis assuming gold talents.

The remarkable part is the king didn't just give this servant some sort of payment plan to pay off the debt over time as the servant had begged for, but forgave the entire astronomical sum!

The Second Servant

Now let's look at the second servant who owed the first servant 100 denarii. A denarius was equal to one day's wages, so that many denarii represented roughly ⅓ of a year's wages.

We have no historical means of determining the worth of a denarius in terms of buying power or its comparative value versus a gold talent, so I'll use another modern statistic for the sake of this discussion.

According to 2020 US census figures, the US median family income is just barely over $63,000/year, roughly $173/day.

Using that figure, it means the second servant owed the first one about $17,300 dollars. While this is a substantial sum well beyond the ability of most Americans to cough up out of savings, it is a trivial sum compared to $6,000,000.

The King

When the king discovered the first servant had harshly treated his coworker over what was chump change by comparison, he was so enraged, he recanted his forgiveness of the first servant's debt and threw him in jail.

Our take-away from this parable is this: after Jesus paid such a horrific price to purchase forgiveness for our vast personal collections of selfish, self-destructive, and harmful-to-others choices, who are we to elevate ourselves to His role as Judge and refuse to forgive those who have committed various sins against us, no matter how heinous those sins may have been?

To put a cherry on this parable sundae: Jesus, God-in-sandals, described the first servant who refused to forgive as "wicked."

Selah!

The World's vs. The Bible's Concept of Forgiveness

Just like everything else we can name, the worldly concept of forgiveness is the polar opposite of the Bible's definition. It's crucial we apply God's definition to this doctrine rather than the world's counterfeit.

Why?

Because if we don't do it God's way, we always fail!

Dictionary (worldly) definition:

ceasing to feel resentment towards an offender.

Bible (God's) definition:

a deliberate choice to abstain from judgment and to trust God's justice towards an offender.

FORGIVENESS IS	FORGIVENESS IS NOT
A feeling	An act of will
Abandonment of justice	Trusting God's justice towards the offender
Trusting the offender	A full pardon
Making ourselves vulnerable to further abuse	What we must do to obtain forgiveness for ourselves
Liking the offender	A commandment of God
Friendship with the offender	An act of faith
Denial (it never happened)	An act of courage
Tolerance (it's OK)	An act requiring God's grace
Forgetting	Crucial to a successful prayer life
Turning the other cheek	Crucial to all present & future relationships
Making a joke of the offense	Trusting God to heal the pain
Politeness or tactfulness	Overcoming evil with good
Passive non-response (stuffing)	The key to freedom

Here's what a highly regarded expert on New Testament Greek has to say on the matter:

> *The word "forgive" is the Greek word* aphiemi, *which means "to permanently dismiss, to liberate completely, to discharge, to send away, or to release." It was used in a secular sense in New Testament times to mean to cancel a debt or to release someone from an obligation of a contract, a commitment, or a promise. Thus, it means forfeiting any right to hold a person captive to a previous commitment or a wrong he has committed. In essence,* aphiemi *is the picture of totally freeing and releasing someone. I like the modern paraphrase of this word: No matter what the offense is, we need to let it go. — Rick Renner*

Forgiveness is a Journey, Not an Event

Sadly, there is a popular misconception within both the Body of Christ and in the secular world that forgiveness is a one-and-done act, rather than a process taking place over time. This causes many to become discouraged and abandon their follow-through when this proves to not be the case and the temptation towards bitterness raises its ugly head at an inopportune moment later down the road. Many who have experienced such disillusionment have thrown up their hands in despair, declaring forgiveness impossible to achieve.

That is *precisely* what Satan wants you to think and do!

The initial choice to forgive is actually the first of many such choices made repeatedly over time, the greater offenses requiring more time and repeated choices than trivial ones.

Each of these choices to forgive involves a simple 1-2-3 process:

1. I will not raise this against you.

This means that I will never bring the offense up again and throw it into your face, no matter how angry I may be at you for either it or whatever else you may do to anger me in the future.

> *To be a Christian means to forgive the inexcusable because God has forgiven the inexcusable in you.*
> C. S. Lewis

Wives, you really need to listen up on this one, because this is a standard tactic you employ during moments of "intense fellowship" with your husbands.

This is especially important for your kids, as well. If your minor child has disobeyed you and you've disciplined him/her for it, never bring it up again. This models God throwing our sins into the "sea of forgetfulness and remembering them no more", thus always giving us a fresh start.

This is for children who are not in the throes of drug/alcohol abuse or other compulsive behaviors. We handle addictions differently, and I do not have the time or space to deal with that topic here.

2. I will not raise it with someone else.

In other words, I will not gossip about you and your offense against me to a third party, such as my buddies (men) or girlfriends (women).

Why is this so important?

Because while we possess the spiritual tools required to deal with the situation through God's grace being more than enough for us to obey Him and not judge the offender, the hearers of your gossip do not have that grace.

If you need to seek worthy counsel from someone who can help you get "unstuck" and need to tell them the gory details, that's OK. Just don't deceive yourself into thinking your best friend who will simply side with you is one of those.

3. I will not raise it again.

This does not mean "forgive and forget" because some offenses are simply too heinous, too traumatic to forget. We remember such offenses for the rest of our lives and usually spend that entire time recovering in various degrees from them.

What it does mean is this: every time the offense comes to mind, I will bring that thought into subjection to the Word of God by choosing to forgive yet again, rather than dwelling on it and rehearsing it repeatedly in my mind, allowing resentment and anger to build. I will continue to make that choice again.

And again.

And again.

And again

Ad nauseam.

One time I was ministering this in a chapel service at the Gospel Rescue Mission Women's & Children's Shelter in Tucson. Every woman present had been a victim of physical, sexual, emotional, and/or verbal abuse. As I covered this last point, I saw the faces of every woman in the room fall and I could sense the tension among them rise.

One of them was bold enough to confront the elephant in the room and blurted out in dismay, "When do we get to stop!?"

The Holy Spirit gave me the perfect answer. I replied, "When that offense no longer has the power to make you angry or put you in pain."

When I said that, everyone relaxed as they saw the goal was indeed attainable, though difficult.

In Summary

One of my favorite maxims is this one:

> *"The important things are always simple.*
> *The simple things are always hard."*

Forgiving offenses — especially the big ones like sexual or physical abuse, rape, or murder of a loved one — is never, ever easy; it *always* requires the grace of God.

Why?

Because God never built us with an innate ability to cope with the sins of others perpetrated against us. Such situations result from living in a fallen world despite God never having created us to live in anything other than a sinless paradise.

Bottom line? If you try to do this using your own strength, you *will* fail!

One of my closest friends is a woman I've known for over 40 years now, though we lost touch with one another for about 17 of them. Prior to our initial introduction and during almost all the hiatus in our friendship — unbeknownst to me until we reconnected — she experienced so many incidents of physical and sexual abuse it is a miracle of God's grace and mercy that she isn't a suicide or in some mental institution somewhere.

If anyone on this planet is qualified to teach a master's class on forgiveness, she is. She penned some words of wisdom I want to share with you:

> *Forgiveness is like a jigsaw puzzle. We have all the pieces and some fit together really quickly. Each time we revisit the puzzle, we see another section, and that comes quickly then — when it was seemingly impossible before. Problem is, the pieces are in a bag, and we can't see them all at once. Otherwise, we might give up, thinking the whole puzzle an impossible feat.*

I hope and pray that when you find yourself in a place where you need to forgive, you will engage in this process with the faith, determination, and persistence needed to recover from it.

And thereby find your freedom!

CHAPTER 16

Unpacking the Lord's Prayer

ATTEND ANY INTER-DENOMINATIONAL gathering of church folks and somewhere along the line, one of the leaders will have the crowd recite the Lord's Prayer, regardless of whether it is direct applicable to the actual proceedings or not.

Why?

Because of its universality among all denominations, most everyone present knows it by heart. That's the up-side.

The down-side is such universality came at a price.

That tragic price was the Lord's Prayer being twisted by traditional denominations into a dead religious work: mindless recitation during a church liturgy and, for Catholics, a tool of penance.

The problem is this: *Jesus never intended it to be used that way!*

Jesus' command was: "In this manner, therefore, pray…," not "Pray these words exactly…"

In other words, Jesus gave it to establish a completely new paradigm for how His followers were to approach Almighty God in prayer. Until Jesus uttered these words, the vast majority of those listening considered God too distant and unapproachable, including His disciples, as do many people, even to this day.

In Matthew's gospel, Jesus taught this prayer in chapter 6 during the Sermon on the Mount. In Luke 11, the disciples came to Jesus, asking Him to teach them how to pray, and He responded with this prayer. It is entirely possible — even likely — that Jesus taught this prayer model on other occasions, though we have no record of it.

Here is Matthew's account:

> *And when you pray, do not use vain repetitions as the heathen do. For they think that they will be heard for their many words. Therefore do not be like them. For your Father knows the things you have need of before you ask Him. In this manner, therefore, pray:*
>
> *Our Father in heaven, hallowed be Your name. Your kingdom come, Your will be done on earth as it is in heaven. Give us this day our daily bread. And forgive us our debts, as we forgive our debtors. And do not lead us into temptation, but deliver us from the evil one. For Yours is the kingdom and the power and the glory forever. Amen. — Matthew 6:7-13*

Vain Repetition

Thayer's Lexicon defines the Greek word "vain repetition" as follows:

vain repetition (*battologeo*)

> *to repeat the same things over and over, to use many idle words, to babble, prate. Some suppose the word derived from Battus, a king of Cyrene, who is said to have stuttered; others from Battus, an author of tedious and wordy poems.*

Why do people do this? Because they have:

- Been taught incorrectly, and/or;
- Assumed their prayers are some sort of recipe, incantation or other dead religious work which is a form of payment in a religious economy.

Dead religious works and religious economies are the very essence of man's religion, all of which have zero resemblance to Christianity.

The Heresy of Penance

In Roman Catholicism, parishioners not only use such vain repetition during the liturgy of a mass, but they must expiate their sins through the heretical concept and practice of penance. Penance is a perfect example of the encroachment of man's religion into Christianity.

Just what is penance, anyway?

According to the Catholic playbook, a priest finds out about the sins committed by his parishioners during their confession. Penance is a series of dead religious works meted out by that priest as a punishment used to redeem themselves from those confessed sins. The reward for performing penance is "absolution" — forgiveness — for those sins, along with priestly permission for them to receive communion.

According to Roman Catholic thinking, the greater the sin(s) in quantity and/or seriousness, the greater penance is required. The frequency and magnitude of sins committed by the feudal lords and knights of

Europe required penances of such enormity that this became one of Pope Urban II's impetuses for the Crusades!

While the concept of receiving healing from confessing our sins to one another is indeed scriptural (James 5:16), we cannot find a single instance in Scripture where our confession must be heard by a priest or any other church official to be valid. Here is just one instance of what the New Testament says on the subject:

> *In Him we have redemption through His blood, the forgiveness of sins, according to the riches of His grace…For by grace you have been saved through faith, and that not of yourselves; it is the gift of God, not of works, lest anyone should boast.— Ephesians 1:7; 2:8-9*

Ergo, it is patently impossible for us to atone for our sins, period.

The blood of Jesus *alone* washes us from our sins, not our dead religious works. We can neither add to nor detract from God's grace through our behavior, good, bad, or indifferent. This is one of the cornerstones of the Protestant Reformation.

> *If we confess our sins, He is faithful and just to forgive us our sins and to cleanse us from all unrighteousness. — 1 John 1:9*

Please note that *nowhere* in this verse — or in any other New Testament passage — will you find the words "priest," "penance," or "absolution" in any passage concerning confession of our sins. In fact, you can perform a word search on the entire Bible and never find the words "penance" or "absolution" anywhere!

- We confess our sins directly to our Heavenly Father, not a priest.
- We receive forgiveness directly from Him personally, with no further action required, I might add. God does expect us to repent, which is a turning away from whatever sin(s) we

are confessing. But repentance is a choice to resubmit to His lordship, rather than a dead religious work designed to curry favor with the Almighty and earn our way back to taking communion. This concept is yet another foundational tenet of the Protestant Reformation.

- Nowhere in the New Testament is a single word said which can be even remotely interpreted to mean our qualification to receive communion depends upon the confession of our sins to any human being, whether priest or layperson.

The idea we need to earn forgiveness through the vain repetition of "Hail Marys" (pure idolatry on its face) and "Our Fathers" (the very topic of this chapter) as prescribed by a so-called "man of God" is a lie from the pit of hell. I genuinely pity the millions of souls deceived by such pernicious false doctrine and held in its bondage.

What About Confessing the Word?

On the Protestant side, quite a few ministers from various denominational traditions think the practice of confessing the Word of God aloud is equally vain repetition.

Not so!

Confessing the Word aloud is 100% scriptural. Here is an example:

> *This Book of the Law shall not depart from your mouth, but* ***you shall meditate in it day and night****, that you may observe to do according to all that is written in it. For then you will make your way prosperous, and then you will have good success.*
>
> —*Joshua 1:8 (emphasis mine)*

meditate (*hagah*)

to moan, growl, utter, muse, mutter, meditate, devise, plot, speak

Such ministers mistakenly assume we are confessing the Word to manipulate God into giving us whatever we want. Some scripturally ignorant people have indeed taken the confessing-the-Word concept and twisted it into this kind of error, but they are a deluded minority.

As I've discussed in Chapters 6, 12, and 13, the scriptural practice of confessing the Word:

- Is always about mind-renewal within ourselves as well as enforcing the will of God using our God-given authority on this earth over the powers of darkness.
- Is never about ordering God around, trying to prove anything to Him, currying favor, or earning brownie points. When warped into the latter, confessing the Word is of absolutely no value to us because it indeed becomes the dead religious work of "vain repetition."

Just because some people don't do it with the right motives and attitude does not negate the principle.

The Lord's Prayer Itself

Our Father in Heaven...

Please note we are addressing God as our Heavenly Father, not as a distant God Almighty. This sets an intimate tone for any prayer we offer. We are coming to our *Abba* — or in the modern vernacular: "Daddy God" (Romans 8:15; Galatians 4:6) — as Jesus exemplified in Mark 14:36. We do so to ask Him for one or more somethings He has already promised to His children.

The second half of the verse is a reminder to ourselves of Who He is in a broader sense. We re-center our minds on Him being the One True God Almighty, who exists outside the space/time continuum.

Therefore, He is never limited by its physical laws and axioms. Neither is He limited by our sinful human nature, with its corrupt motivations and finite intellectual capacity.

Hallowed Be Your Name...

There are a couple of aspects to this. The first is holding the name of God in reverence, as directed in Commandment #3:

> *You shall not take the name of the Lord your God in vain, for the Lord will not hold him guiltless who takes His name in vain. — Exodus 20:7*

The second aspect is that of worship. Worship sets our priorities by establishing at the outset of our prayers only He is worthy of honor, only He deserves glory, only He is qualified to receive our veneration, devotion, and worship.

Worship refocuses our minds on who is in charge and whom we serve, ever reminding us we are God's servants, not the other way around. He is neither a cosmic bellhop we command to give us stuff nor is He a supernatural "Get Out Of Jail Free" card we can call upon only when we need Him to bail us out of our self-inflicted jams.

Your Kingdom Come, Your Will be Done on Earth as it is in Heaven...

Most people recite this phrase as two separate thoughts or concepts:

1. Your kingdom come (full stop)
2. Your will be done on earth as it is in heaven (full stop).

Actually, they are one continuous thought with the latter phrase amplifying the meaning of the first.

This verse is cram-packed with implications. First, Jesus says that we should pray for God's Kingdom to be established on the earth.

This completely torpedoes the bogus precept of "absolute sovereignty" as preached by Calvinists and Roman Catholicism. As we covered in Chapters 6 and 7, God is indeed sovereign, but has limited His sovereignty by His own choice through both His delegation of some authority to men and what He has proclaimed in His Word. We are currently soldiers of God in a war between the kingdom of darkness and the Kingdom of God over this planet. Therefore, not everything happening here is at God's direction and causation. Here's the logical conundrum:

> *If God was indeed absolute ruler of this planet, why would God-in-Sandals command us to pray for a kingdom to come which is already in place?*

So we are to pray for God's reign to be established on this earth. Then Jesus gives us a yardstick to measure how much of that reign actually exists: wherever God's will is being done on earth in the same manner and to the same degree as His will is being done in heaven.

Where does that "will being done here on earth" begin?

You guessed it! With us!

Jesus Himself said it:

> *Now having been questioned by the Pharisees as to when the kingdom of God was coming, He answered them and said, "The kingdom of God is not coming with signs to be observed; nor will they say, 'Look, here it is!' or 'There it is!' For behold,* ***the kingdom of God is within you.****" — Luke 17:20-21 (emphasis mine)*

Jesus pointed the Pharisees to a critical fact: the Kingdom of God is not a governmental entity they could discern through the existence of an earthly king who enforces his political boundaries by force of arms.

Rather, it is a spiritual kingdom located in the hearts of those who lovingly submit to King Jesus. That submission leads them to die to themselves and their own desires/ambitions. In other words, they follow Him.

If we are going to do God's will on earth the same way it's being done in heaven, we need to take a long, hard look at how His will is being done there so we'll know how well we're doing here.

When God orders His angels to do something:

- How rapidly do they respond?
- How thoroughly do they carry out His instructions?
- How accurately do they do what is commanded of them?
- How frequently is He obeyed?
- With what attitude do the angels respond?
- Does God have to cajole, persuade or argue with them to obtain their obedience?

Using these criteria, we can now complete our definition:

> *The Kingdom of God is located in the human hearts of those who do His will on earth instantly, thoroughly, precisely, constantly, enthusiastically, and without argument or resistance.*

Now can we Christ-followers ever do this perfectly?

No way! If we could, Jesus would have died needlessly.

All we can do is aspire to it by allowing God's Word to progressively change us by His grace into looking, acting, and reacting more and more like Jesus. He is the only human who perfectly obeyed the Heavenly Father while walking this planet . The $10 theological word for that process is "sanctification."

This isn't just about God's kingdom coming to others. When we pray for God's reign to come to this earth, we are in fact submitting ourselves to His lordship and asking for it to extend through ourselves to others as we obey Him.

Give Us This Day Our Daily Bread...

This is simply a request for God's daily provision. God doesn't promise us we will "arrive" at some level of provision where we no longer need to depend upon Him. What He promises throughout His Word is, this: if we will put Him first and operate in His wisdom and generosity, we will always have enough to meet our own needs and be generous to others. In other words, He expects us to ask Him for it, not merely assume it will happen automagically.

And Forgive Us Our Debts, As We Forgive Our Debtors...

Or more precisely: "And forgive us our sins, as we forgive those who have sinned against us."

As we've already thoroughly discussed in the previous chapter, here is Jesus yet again calling us to forgive those who have selfishly violated our boundaries and harmed us physically, emotionally, or professionally.

Here again we see the word "as," meaning "to the same extent and in the same manner." This is the law of sowing and reaping in action: to the extent and with the same manner that we forgive, we reap forgiveness from our Heavenly Father.

And Lead Us Not Into Temptation, But Deliver Us From Evil...

Many subconsciously interpret the classic wording of this verse as meaning we must actively pray for God not to lead us into sin else He will. That is totally bogus.

Here is this same verse in a few different translations:

Keep us from being tempted and protect us from evil. — CEV

And don't let us yield to temptation, but rescue us from the evil one. — NLT

Keep us safe from ourselves and the Devil. — MSG

In reality, we are praying for God to lead us away from temptation and rescue us from evil or the Evil One. It places a humble demand upon His freely given and limitless grace because it is only by His grace we are able to resist temptations and endure trials. It also brings to our conscious minds the salient fact we cannot defeat the devil using our own strength; we desperately require divine intervention and empowerment for us to be victorious.

For Yours is the Kingdom and the Power and the Glory Forever.

Some translations leave this out because of differences in the original manuscripts. Regardless, it is yet another affirmation that God is in charge, He is all-powerful, and He deserves all the glory.

Amen

This is yet another word used in our prayers with the vast majority of us having no clue as to what it actually means. Most folks treat the word "amen" like what some jokingly call The Holy Sign-off:

"In Jesus' name, Amen."

The Greek word is a direct carry-over of the Hebrew.

amen

so it is, so be it, may it be fulfilled

Thayer's Greek Lexicon further states:

> *"It was a custom, which passed over from the synagogues to the Christian assemblies, that when he who had read or discoursed, had offered up solemn prayer to God, the others responded "amen," and* ***thus made the substance of what was uttered their own."*** *(emphasis mine)*

Amen!

CHAPTER

17

Giving Thanks

ONE CONCEPT INSEPARABLY LINKED TO prayer throughout the Bible is our expressing gratitude to God. Earlier in this book, I cited a pair of Scripture verses concerning prayer which also mentioned thanksgiving. I want to share them with you again here:

> *Continue earnestly in prayer,* ***being vigilant in it with thanksgiving…*** *— Colossians 4:2 (emphasis mine)*

> *Rejoice always, pray without ceasing,* ***in everything give thanks;*** *for this is the will of God in Christ Jesus for you.*
>
> *— 1 Thessalonians 5:16-18 (emphasis mine)*

Let's add a couple more:

> *Therefore I exhort first of all that supplications, prayers, intercessions, and* ***giving of thanks*** *be made for all men…*
>
> *— 1 Timothy 2:1 (emphasis mine)*

> *Therefore by Him let us continually offer the sacrifice of praise to God, that is, the fruit of our lips,* ***giving thanks to His name.***
> *— Hebrews 13:15 (emphasis mine)*

As you can see, God inextricably links the practice of prayer with our giving thanks to Him. Any prayer life consistently excluding thanksgiving will quickly devolve into our demanding things of Him with a sense of entitlement, an attitude God neither appreciates nor will honor.

We can express our thankfulness for things ranging from the significant and/or supernatural such as our salvation, healing, and financial provision to the comparatively mundane, such as our appreciation of a beautiful day, an amazing sunset, or the cute things our kids do and say — and everywhere in between.

Let's explore this idea in depth.

Theology Reset!

Out With the Old

As you are reading this, you are witnessing someone who has undergone a personal theology shift. For literally decades, ministers had taught me — and in turn, I had taught others — that passage in 1 Thessalonians cited above makes a crucial distinction concerning thankfulness: it says "in," not "for."

Therefore, we are *never* to be thankful for:

- The attacks of Satan
- The sins of other people against us or others, or;
- The problems, challenges, or disasters resulting from our living in a lost, fallen, and decaying world

Instead, we are to be thankful to Him for what He has already done.

- He has saved us from the power of sin, death, and hell
- He's made us righteous in His sight by the blood of Jesus
- He gave us His Holy Spirit to live inside us
- He healed us physically and mentally
- He delivered us from poverty
- He put His love in our hearts by the Holy Spirit
- He's made us victorious over the powers of darkness
- He redeems the sins of others and the other trials we face in this world, working them together for good
- Etc., etc.

The practical outworking of this theological stance is this: amid our trials and temptations and as we are praying against them, we are to maintain an attitude of gratitude towards God for all He has accomplished in our lives but never for the temptations and trials themselves.

In With the New

As I was researching to prepare for this book, I came across another passage in Ephesians:

> *Therefore do not be unwise, but understand what the will of the Lord is. And do not be drunk with wine, in which is dissipation; but be filled with the Spirit, speaking to one another in psalms and hymns and spiritual songs, singing and making melody in your heart to the Lord,* ***giving thanks always for all things*** *to God the Father in the name of our Lord Jesus Christ, submitting to one another in the fear of God. —Ephesians 5:17-21 (emphasis mine)*

Please note in the boldfaced text of this verse it uses the word "for" not "in." The Greek word "for" (*hupo*) means precisely that and nowhere else in the New Testament is *hupo* ever translated as "in." And "all" means precisely that: *all, without exception.* No matter how hard I tried, I could not reconcile this verse with my previous theology on the subject.

Danger! Danger, Will Robinson! <sirens blare, warning lights flash> *Attempted theological square peg insertion into scriptural round hole alert!*

What's a believer — even a minister and theologian — supposed to do when the Bible contradicts his theology? The answer is simple, but difficult: *adjust his theology to conform to the Scriptures!*

What are the implications of this change? Does it completely negate my extensive body of writings dedicated to refuting the Calvinist/Catholic error portraying God as a cosmic child-abuser who visits pain, calamity, loss, destruction, and death in order to teach us something? Actually, *not at all!*

Here are some other significant passages we need to consider:

> *My brethren, count it all joy when you fall into various trials, knowing that the testing of your faith produces patience. But let patience have its perfect work, that you may be perfect and complete, lacking nothing. —James 1:2–4*
>
> *But thanks be to God, who gives us the victory through our Lord Jesus Christ. — 1 Corinthians 15:57*
>
> *Now thanks be to God who always leads us in triumph in Christ, and through us diffuses the fragrance of His knowledge in every place. — 2 Corinthians 2:14*
>
> *For whatever is born of God overcomes the world. And this is the victory that has overcome the world — our faith. — 1 John 5:4*

Here is what I now believe to be a theologically sound viewpoint concerning thanksgiving and trials:

- We continue to never, *ever* attribute the trials in our lives to God.
- Instead, we thank Him not only for the wonderful things in our lives but also for the current challenges we face. Why? Because they are opportunities for Him to show Himself strong on our behalf.
- We do this knowing in advance He has given us surpassing victory over them through the finished work of Jesus' death, burial, and resurrection. In summary, the Cross and the Resurrection trump all!

Because of all that, we can rejoice amid the trials, tribulations, and disasters we may face, knowing the faith and patience we develop during that process will stand us in good stead when facing future challenges.

When it is all said and done — if we persevere by His grace — we win! We may be bloodied — even scarred — but we are ultimately victorious in this life.

Thanksgiving is Our Faith's Partner

Why do I say this? Because our thanksgiving is a crucial element in supporting our faith. Here's what I mean:

Assume I've promised you something. For you to thank me for it *before* you've actually received it, you *must* have a reasonable assurance in your heart and mind that I will, in fact, give it to you.

Whenever we thank God for something we're praying for as we pray for it, that act automatically puts us into an assumption we will receive it. The bottom line is it keeps our faith on track and focused on God's faithfulness to honor His promises.

That *never* means we thank God to manipulate Him into doing something. Thanksgiving comes from our heart of gratitude towards our gracious Father — it should *never* become a tool of entitlement. That assumption concept I mentioned in the last paragraph has to do with our mind renewal process (remember Chapter 13?) which aligns our hearts and minds with His.

Ask Once, Thank Many

Many verses imply we should persist in prayer over an issue. Yet doesn't that very requirement for persistence cause our minds to call into question whether we will indeed receive it? Or cause us to think we need to pray until we reach some unknown-to-us-but-known-to-God level of achievement earning us an answer to our prayers?

The former mind-set brings doubt to our minds, and the latter causes us to approach God based on our dead religious works, rather than by His grace.

As we covered in Chapter 12, God has already given us everything we need in the spirit realm, and done so generously beyond our capacity to imagine. He does not have to be persuaded, cajoled, or otherwise "talked into" answering our prayers. As it says in Romans:

> *What then shall we say to these things? If God is for us, who can be against us? He who did not spare His own Son, but delivered Him up for us all,* ***how shall He not with Him also freely give us all things?*** *— Romans 8:31-32 (emphasis mine)*

We are not in the business of persuading God to give us something through our puny human efforts at being pious, religious, or zealous, but allowing God's Word to renew our minds to the fact whatever we are praying for is already ours through the finished work of the Cross.

It is the world, our flesh, and the devil who oppose that fact, trying to rob us of what is ours.

The solution I've discovered over the years is the concept of "ask once, thank many." That means that at the outset, I pray and ask God for whatever it is I'm requesting of Him, receiving it as my own according to Mark 11:24 and thanking Him for the result at the outset. From then on, until the answer manifests, I'm in thanksgiving mode, always thanking God for His answer to that prayer.

Putting Faith & Thanksgiving Together

Here we have yet another Scripture inextricably linking prayer to thanksgiving. I saved this one until last, rather than lumping it with the rest of the verses quoted above, because I wanted to delve into this one in depth. This is an old friend from earlier in this book:

> *Be anxious for nothing, but in everything by prayer and supplication, with thanksgiving, let your requests be made known to God; and the peace of God, which surpasses all understanding, will guard your hearts and minds through Christ Jesus.*
>
> *Finally, brethren, whatever things are true, whatever things are noble, whatever things are just, whatever things are pure, whatever things are lovely, whatever things are of good report, if there is any virtue and if there is anything praiseworthy — meditate on these things. — Philippians 4:6-8*

Let's unpack this, starting with a look at some Greek definitions for key terms used in the passage.

anxious (*merimnao*)

> *to be anxious, to be troubled with cares, to care for, look out for (a thing), to seek to promote one's interests, caring or providing for*

nothing (*medeis*)

nobody, no one, nothing

everything (*pas*)

each, every, any, all, the whole, everyone, all things, everything

peace (*eirene*)

a state of national tranquillity, exemption from the rage and havoc of war, peace between individuals, i.e. harmony, concord, security, safety, prosperity, felicity, (because peace and harmony make and keep things safe and prosperous)

of the Messiah's peace: the way that leads to peace (salvation)

of Christianity: the tranquil state of a soul assured of its salvation through Christ, and so fearing nothing from God and content with its earthly lot, of whatsoever sort that is

the blessed state of devout and upright men after death

surpasses (*huperecho*)

to excel, to be superior, better than, to surpass

understanding (*nous*)

the mind, comprising alike the faculties of perceiving and understanding and those of feeling, judging, determining; the intellectual faculty, the understanding; reason in the narrower sense, as the capacity for spiritual truth, the higher powers of the soul, the faculty of perceiving divine things, of recognizing goodness and of hating evil; the power of considering and judging soberly, calmly and impartially; a particular mode of thinking and judging, i.e thoughts, feelings, purposes, desires

guard (*phroureo*)

to guard, protect by a military guard, by watching and guarding to preserve one for the attainment of something

meditate (*logizomai*)

> *to reckon, count, compute, calculate, count over; to take into account, to make an account of; to gather or infer; to consider, take into account, weigh, meditate on; to suppose, deem, judge.*
>
> *Logizomai deals with facts, not suppositions or assumptions. If I logizomai that I have X amount of money in my bank account, I actually have X amount in my bank account.*

Using these definitions, let's construct our own home-brew "Amplified Version" translation of this passage:

> *Do not be anxious, fearful, fretful, troubled with cares, or promoting your own self-interests for anyone or anything, but in everything without exception by prayer and supplication, with thanksgiving, make your requests and petitions known to God; and the peace of God [that state of tranquility of a soul assured of its salvation through Christ, and so fearing nothing from God and content with its earthly lot, of whatever sort that is, that peace] which far surpasses our limited human ability to understand [comprehend or grasp intellectually], will mount guard over and protect your hearts and minds through Christ Jesus.*
>
> *Finally, brethren, whatever things are true, whatever things are of godly and honorable character, whatever things are holy and righteous, whatever things are pure and free of carnality and every fault, whatever things are acceptable and pleasing, whatever things are spoken well of, if there is any moral excellence and if there is anything worthy of commendation or praise — consider and act on these things as your true reality, whether or not you can see them.*

Since our expanded version of verse 8 above defines the very essence of both faith and godly character, we can see in this one 3-verse passage the integration of prayer, thanksgiving, and faith and how they cooperate together in affirming God and His Word as the Answer to our earthly and spiritual needs.

CHAPTER

18

The Beauty of Worship

GOD HAS USED ANIMALS TO TEACH ME things on multiple occasions. In this chapter, we're going to dig into one such lesson. Please bear with me as I share some personal information, because it's crucial to the point I believe God wants me to make.

I've owned cats (aka Mobile Dust-Bunny Generators) for almost my entire life and am a dyed-in-the-fur cat lover. All you dog lovers just collectively groaned inwardly and thought, *"Oh, no! He's one of them!"* Not to worry, we're actually going to talk more about dogs than cats. I can imagine those of you who just groaned are now completely confused. Bear with me. You'll love this!

One of my previous beasts was a long-haired orange tabby mutt-cat with golden eyes. In a fit of originality, I named him "Tiger." He was a 15-pound neutered tom who definitely had some Maine Coon DNA in him, because he had a dense triple-layer fur coat and huge snowshoe feet. He was also the scruffiest cat I've ever seen, hence his two of his

nicknames: Mr. Scruffy and Rumpledcatskin.

I was his human since he was about 8 weeks old, when I adopted both him and his fraternal twin-brother Simba, a pure-white domestic shorthair. Tiger's only direct contact with other animals for his entire life was Simba and Catchou, our blue lynx-point Siamese.

Nothing particularly noteworthy so far.

What made Tiger unique was he thought he was a dog. While he had all the physical attributes of a cat, he definitely thought and acted like a dog. Examples? He slavishly adored me, was aggressively affectionate, was jealous of my wife when she cuddled with me, played fetch (he taught himself!), immediately came when I called him, and could not stand to be much farther than a few feet away from me, if that far, ever.

The absolute #1 top priority on his personal agenda was this: *to be in Daddy's presence and receive his touch!* This is what Tiger lived for, what he craved way above and beyond his normal kitty needs for food, water, and a clean litter box. That cat absolutely adored me. He literally jumped at every opportunity to express it with a complete disregard for my personal space or situational appropriateness — and express it aggressively, I might add!

He usually resolved his attention deficits whenever I sat in my recliner to pray or watch TV. The second my butt hit the seat, he was immediately in my lap, with a slavish "I love you" look I jokingly refer to as "the adoration of the cat eye." He kneaded my belly with his front paws, stabbing me with his claws, and performed head-butts and shoulder-dives in an orgy of feline greeting behaviors, all the while purring as hard as he could. All the while, he was talking to me in his whiny little voice, telling me how much he loved me, as well as all about his kitty problems.

This is where he got one of his other nicknames: Daddy's Pest.

You could always see what he was thinking by the look written all over his face: *I'm with Daddy and all is right in my fuzzy little world!*

Those of you who own dogs have experienced this same intense devotion/adoration and your fur-babies' compulsive need to be with you. They sleep on your beds, sit in your laps, and jump up on you, wagging their tails when you return from wherever you just went. Your performance or lack thereof is never of concern to them.

In their view, you hang the moon and the stars!

True Worshippers

For years, I found all this aggressive attention to be annoying, especially when Tiger kept pushing Simba out of the way to get to me. But eventually, I finally "got" what God was trying to show me through him:

Tiger was a true worshipper!

What I mean by "true" is he was the genuine article. I was his *raison d'être* and his existence revolved around worshipping Daddy. Yes, he did other normal kitty stuff — eating, drinking, playing with Simba and Catchou, etc. — but whenever I was available, he dropped everything else and I became the sometimes-reluctant focus of his undivided attention.

God knew I would never willingly own a dog, so He arranged for me to have a cat who would teach me the same lesson any dog owner would immediately grasp.

His Presence is the Difference

A former pastor of mine mentors other pastors throughout Northern Mexico. As he was discussing worship with one of them during one of his trips, the Mexican pastor exclaimed, *"¡La presencia de Dios es la diferencia!"* The translation is precisely what you would expect: "God's presence is the difference!"

> *You will show me the path of life; In Your presence is fullness of joy; at Your right hand are pleasures forevermore. — Psalm 16:11*

If we are worshipping for *any* reason other than to enter God's presence, *we've missed the point and missed it badly.*

My Personal History with Worship

Years ago, in my previous ignorance on this topic, I had the same attitude held by many church-goers concerning the musical portion of a service: it was just the warm-up to give us something to do before what really counted: the Word of God and the sermon! So I would consistently show up for church late, usually wandering in about halfway through the song service.

Then God corrected my thinking through some excellent teaching on worship. What an eye opener!

Through my bullheadedness and ignorance of the Scriptures, I had been depriving myself for years of experiencing God's presence and the joys of true worship. Now the song service is crucial to me, rather than an optional throwaway I can take or leave.

I need Daddy God's presence!

The Biggest Reason for Worship

> *I beseech you therefore, brethren, by the mercies of God, that you present your bodies a living sacrifice, holy, acceptable to God, which is* ***your reasonable service*** *— Romans 12:1 (emphasis mine)*

That boldfaced phrase is *logikos latreia* in the Greek. Here's how other versions and resources translate those two words:

reasonable service (*logikos latreia*)

spiritual service of worship —NASB

spiritual act of worship — NIV

a reasonable act of worship — WEY

spiritual worship — RSV

reasonable (rational, intelligent) service & spiritual worship — AMP

reasonable sacred services — Thayer's Greek Lexicon

Worship is our only reasonable and appropriate response to God's gift of Jesus on the cross. After all He has given us, who are we to be unappreciative of Who He is and thankful for what He's done?

Worship vs. Thanksgiving

While thanksgiving can and certainly is an integral part of our worshipping God, there *is* a difference:

- Thanksgiving is about what God has done in and for us and for others.
- Worship is about Who He is, specifically His character and divine attributes.

Whenever we worship, it's not about anything having to do with us, but it's everything having to do with Him.

What are the attributes and character of God? Well, I made a fairly comprehensive list in one of my blog articles entitled "*Who's In Charge? The Cosmic Battle For Control*" listed in this book's Appendix for starters. All of those and whatever else you discover from God's Word are definitely in play here.

We worship God for being holy, loving, just, faithful, almighty, redemptive, merciful, and gracious, just for starters. One phrase frequently cited where the Old Testament described certain Jews as worshipping God in the beauty of holiness is *"The Lord is good! And His mercy endures forever!"*

The Foundation of Worship

Hardly any verses exist in the New Testament concerning worship. Why is this? Because anything we find in the Old Testament which the New Testament has not superseded simply carries over intact. Accordingly, most of the Scripture references we'll be using are from the Old Testament.

Back when the Seventh-Day Adventist cult got started, they made a big deal out of worshipping on the Jewish Sabbath instead of Sunday, like everyone else. There was, of course, a great deal of push-back by the pietists within Christendom who wanted to stick to the traditional Sunday services.

Both missed the point entirely: *we should worship God every day!*

Worship's Foundation is Humble Submission

All true worship, like prayer, starts with us humbling ourselves in submission to the lordship of Jesus Christ — not just when we initially received salvation, but during our ongoing sanctification. It means that we are:

- Actively abandoning earthly idols to serve the One True God.
- Promptly responding in obedience with a good heart to things God has told us to do and not to do.
- Prioritizing time with Him in prayer and the Word in our daily lives.
- Not hardening our hearts in unforgiveness and resentment towards those who have wronged us.
- Not judging as "less than" those devoted to a lifestyle or doctrinal position we disagree with.
- Actively engaging in our love relationship with the Most High God, rather than Him being a religious accessory to our lives that we pull out and dust off only on Sundays.

Please note I presented this list in the what the Greek language calls the continuous perfect tense. In other words, we are talking about our ongoing process of sanctification, not some lofty hurdle we must clear before we can qualify as worshippers.

In summary, the vast majority of churchgoers in the US are not experiencing — and will not experience short of a major revival in their hearts — true worship.

Why?

Because worship is a lifestyle flowing out of our love relationship with Jesus, not a religious act we do only on Sundays in a church service. Here's what Jesus said on the matter:

> *These people draw near to Me with their mouth, and honor Me with their lips, but their heart is far from Me. And in vain*

> *they worship Me, teaching as doctrines the commandments of men. — Matthew 15:8-9*

Worship is an Act of Surrender

Interestingly, the only worship posture mentioned in both Old and New Testaments is raising our hands:

> *Lift up your hands in the sanctuary, and bless the Lord.*
> *— Psalm 134:2*

> *I desire therefore that the men pray everywhere, lifting up holy hands, without wrath and doubting; — 1 Timothy 2:8*

What's the significance of this? In every culture and society on this planet, *raising one's hands is universally a sign of surrender.*

Our daily abject surrender to the lordship of Jesus Christ in our lives is what He expects from a worshipper.

We despise sycophants and brown-nosers, people who kiss up to the boss to curry favor but secretly despise him or her. Such folks are the first to stab that boss in the back, given a suitable opportunity. Are we really so delusional to think the omniscient God of the Universe — who knows the heart and mind of every human — will not recognize when we're faking submission to Him?

> *Has the Lord as great delight in burnt offerings and sacrifices as in obeying the voice of the Lord? Behold, to obey is better than sacrifice and to heed than the fat of rams. For rebellion is as the sin of witchcraft and stubbornness is as iniquity and idolatry… — 1 Samuel 15:22-23a*

The bottom line is this: if we have not submitted to Him,

- We can try to worship

- We can simulate worship
- We can pretend to worship
- We can appear to worship

But all we're really doing is going through the motions, wasting precious time and good air!

Our Worship is Loud

While God is perfectly willing to receive worship at any volume level our circumstances and boldness permit, the consistent thread running throughout Old Testament worship is this: *rowdy and unrestrained abandon* devoid of any concern for what other people may think about us.

> *Praise Him for His mighty acts; praise Him according to His excellent greatness! — Psalm 150:2*

The Hebrew word for "praise" used in this verse is the word *halal.*

praise (*halal*)

> *to shine, to be boastful of God, to make a fool of oneself, to act like a madman*

This word coupled with the suffix -yah — meaning God — is where we get the word *hallelujah*: praise God.

As you can see, this kind of behavior is a far cry from what we see in most Minority World church services outside of the charismatic and black communities.

Why is that?

I believe the words "according to" in this verse implies the concept of "in proportion to." We can safely retranslate this phrase as saying "praise Him in proportion to His excellent greatness." From this, I believe we can establish a fundamental truism:

> *The fervency of our worship is directly proportional to how much we perceive His excellent greatness.*

Jesus Himself confirms this concept with the following verse contextually tied to the concept of worship:

> *Therefore I say to you, her sins, which are many, are forgiven, for she loved much. But to whom little is forgiven, the same loves little. — Luke 7:47*

All this then begs the question:

How big is your God?

The Role of Music

God Created It

> *Where were you when I laid the foundations of the earth? Tell Me, if you have understanding. Who determined its measurements? Surely you know! Or who stretched the line upon it? To what were its foundations fastened? Or who laid its cornerstone,* ***when the morning stars sang together, and all the sons of God shouted for joy?*** *— Job 38:4-7 (emphasis mine)*

The Hebrew word for "sang" in verse 7 is the word *ranan* and the word for "shouted" is *ruah*:

sang (ranan)
to sing for joy, to shout joyfully, to give a ringing cry, to rejoice

shouted (ruah)
to shout in triumph, to shout for joy, an ear-splitting noise

Again, the concept of rowdiness in worship rears its head!

Heaven's Former Worship Leader

Music is so important to God, He created a special being just to lead worship in heaven:

> *How you are fallen from heaven, O Lucifer, son of the morning!... —Isaiah 14:12a*

The name "Lucifer" literally means "light bearer" and comes from the root word *halal* we've already discussed earlier. Another verse gives us further insight:

> *...Thus says the Lord GOD: "You were the seal of perfection, Full of wisdom and perfect in beauty. You were in Eden, the garden of God; Every precious stone was your covering: the sardius, topaz, and diamond, beryl, onyx, and jasper, sapphire, turquoise, and emerald with gold. The workmanship of your timbrels and pipes was prepared for you on the day you were created. —Ezekiel 28:12b–13*

Virtually every Bible scholar agrees this passage is a description of Lucifer, although Ezekiel appears to be addressing the King of Tyre. The last half of verse 13 implies his body actually has music instruments built into it.

Then Lucifer rebelled, thus becoming Satan and we know the rest.

Music is a Spiritual Force

> *And the Lord said to Moses:..."Now therefore, write down this song for yourselves, and teach it to the children of Israel; put it in their mouths, that this song may be a witness for Me against the children of Israel. When I have brought them to the land flowing with milk and honey, of which I swore to their fathers, and they*

> *have eaten and filled themselves and grown fat, then they will turn to other gods and serve them; and they will provoke Me and break My covenant. Then it shall be, when many evils and troubles have come upon them, that this song will testify against them as a witness; for it will not be forgotten in the mouths of their descendants, for I know the inclination of their behavior today, even before I have brought them to the land of which I swore to give them." Therefore Moses wrote this song the same day, and taught it to the children of Israel. — Deuteronomy 31:19-22*

Music is a spiritual force designed by God to carry a message straight into our hearts. Modern medical science proves this through brain scans which have shown music is the one activity using both hemispheres of the brain simultaneously.

Satan knows this better than anyone but God Himself. It is his intrinsic link to music driving him to dominate the secular music industry and direct its content towards idolatry, sin, arrogance, violence, self-seeking, and rebellion against authority. Here's just a few obvious samples of his successes to date:

Sympathy For The Devil — The Rolling Stones

Running With The Devil — Van Halen

Black Magic Woman — Santana

Witchy Woman — The Eagles

Highway To Hell — AC/DC

Fire — Arthur Brown

Hellhound On My Trail — Robert Johnson

I'm OK — Styx

The Rites of Spring — Igor Stravinsky

In the Hall of the Mountain King — Edvard Grieg

This list doesn't even begin to include a host of musical compositions — and even entire genres, like death metal and gangsta rap — all of which exalt the worst Hell has to offer.

Because of this, musicians — Christian and non-Christian alike — have a huge spiritual target painted on their chests and are especially vulnerable to pride, arrogance, and rebellion, because the enemy knows precisely how to push their buttons. This correlates to the recent deconversions of several worship leaders from US mega-churches.

Music: A Blessing From God

> *Gladness is taken away, And joy from the plentiful field; In the vineyards there will be no singing, nor will there be shouting; No treaders will tread out wine in the presses; I have made their shouting cease. — Isaiah 16:10*

The context of this verse is God pronouncing judgment over the nation of Moab for their arrogance and idolatry. Part of what God invokes over them is a removal of song, so we can legitimately state that God views someone not having music as being accursed.

Jesus Sings With Us

> *For both He who sanctifies and those who are being sanctified are all of one, for which reason He is not ashamed to call them brethren, saying: "I will declare Your name to My brethren; in the midst of the assembly I will sing praise to You. — Hebrews 2:11-12*

Various Methods of Worship

Raising Your Hands

We've already touched on this one earlier, but I would like to cite one more verse on this:

> *Surely the righteous shall give thanks to Your name; the upright shall dwell in Your presence. — Psalm 140:13*

The Hebrew word for "give thanks" in this verse is *yawdah*:

give thanks (*yawdah*)

to raise the hands in thanksgiving and give loud praise

Sing, Shout & Give Thanks

> *Oh come, let us sing to the Lord! Let us shout joyfully to the Rock of our salvation. Let us come before His presence with thanksgiving; Let us shout joyfully to Him with psalms. — Psalm 95:1-2*

The Hebrew words for "sing" and "shout" are the words *ranan* and *ruah*, respectively, both of which we've already discussed earlier in this chapter. The word I want to point out to you here is a new word for "thanksgiving:" *towdah*:

thanksgiving (*towdah*)

to stretch out the hand in agreement, to offer a sacrifice of thanksgiving

A related word not used in this passage, but elsewhere:

tehillah

to sing a song or hymn of praise

Prostrating Yourself

shachah

to bow down, to prostrate oneself before a king or ruler

The vast majority of the words translated as "worship" in the Old Testament are this word. The New Testament Greek word *proskuneo*, universally translated as "worship," describes the same posture.

Here again, we see the concept of submission to His authority baked into the scriptures cake of worship.

Giving a Mighty Shout

> *Blessed are the people who know the joyful sound! They walk, O Lord, in the light of Your countenance. In Your name they rejoice all day long, And in Your righteousness they are exalted.*
>
> — *Psalm 89:15-16*

joyful sound (*teruah*)

a mighty shout of joy or war

Teruah is a more powerful form of the already-discussed *ruah*. They translate this word as a "great shout" at the battle of Jericho recorded in the Book of Joshua.

Giving in an Offering

asah

to make an offering

If you've ever questioned the legitimacy of pre-offering sermonettes depicting financial giving as an act of worship, this should lay that concern to rest.

Playing Musical Instruments

zamar

to praise by playing an instrument

For others who have questioned whether an instrumental solo during a worship service was truly worship or just the musician showing off, this also should put that issue to rest.

Related to this is whether it's scriptural for a song service to be accompanied by musical instruments at all, rather than sung *a cappella*. This word plus a multitude of verses found throughout the Book of Psalms should resolve that debate once and for all.

Laughing & Expressing Joy

sashaq

to laugh, rejoice, make merry

samach

to rejoice, to be gladden

For those of you who have wondered whether "laughing in the Spirit" is of God or not, those two words should answer that question.

Dancing

> *Let them praise His name with the dance; Let hem sing praises to Him with the timbrel and harp. — Psalm 149:3*

> *Praise Him with the timbrel and dance; Praise Him with stringed instruments and flutes! — Psalm 150:4*

dance (*machowl*)

dancing: from the Hebrew word chuwl

chuwl

dance; to twist, writhe; to whirl about

This leads us to the occasion where David — who God Himself described as a man after His own heart — danced before the Lord at the restoration of the Ark of the Covenant to Israel from its prior captivity by the Philistines:

> *Then David danced before the Lord with all his might; and David was wearing a linen ephod… Now as the ark of the Lord came into the City of David, Michal, Saul's daughter, looked*

through a window and saw King David leaping and whirling before the Lord… —2 Samuel 6:14,16

dancing (*karar*)

dance; to whirl about

leaping (*pazaz*)

to be nimble; to leap, show agility

What we have here is David publicly whirling and dancing with pizzazz (sorry, the pun was too tempting to resist) before God literally in his underwear. When his wife, Saul's daughter Michal, saw him, she despised him for what she later described as a total lack of kingly propriety and dignity.

Upon David's return to the palace to bless his family, he was completely unrepentant of his actions and not only rubbed her nose in the fact God had chosen him over her father, but informed her how, given similar circumstances in the future, he'd do it all over again.

Interestingly, the historian writing this account recorded that, after her tantrum, she never bore another child until the day she died. Whether that was due to divine judgment or David refusing to lie with her, the Bible doesn't specify.

But this story carries an important warning for those who would judge others as "less than" for uninhibited worship behavior. *Selah!*

Worship is Physical

Please note how none of these descriptions of worship in the Bible bear even the slightest resemblance to the rigid, stodgy, passive, and stoic song services found in the vast majority of American and European denominational congregations on any given Sunday morning.

None of these words denote passive attitudes, mental mind-sets, or thought patterns. *They are all specific acts we perform or postures we assume with our physical bodies.*

What we do with our bodies changes the way we feel and think. This is why energetic worship is a great weapon against depression.

God Shows Up When We Worship Him

> *But You are holy, enthroned in the praises of Israel. — Psalm 22:3*

> *And it came to pass when the priests came out of the Most Holy Place (for all the priests who were present had sanctified themselves, without keeping to their divisions), and the Levites who were the singers, all those of Asaph and Heman and Jeduthun, with their sons and their brethren, stood at the east end of the altar, clothed in white linen, having cymbals, stringed instruments and harps, and with them one hundred and twenty priests sounding with trumpets — indeed it came to pass, when the trumpeters and singers were as one, to make one sound to be heard in praising and thanking the Lord, and when they lifted up their voice with the trumpets and cymbals and instruments of music, and praised the Lord, saying: "For He is good, For His mercy endures forever," that the house, the house of the Lord, was filled with a cloud, so that the priests could not continue ministering because of the cloud; for the glory of the Lord filled the house of God. — 2 Chronicles 5:11*

What is the value of God's presence? In His presence:

There is Fullness of Joy

> *You will show me the path of life; in Your presence is fullness of joy; at Your right hand are pleasures forevermore. — Psalm 16:11*

There is Power

The mountains melt like wax at the presence of the Lord. At the presence of the Lord of the whole earth, the heavens declare His righteousness, and all the peoples see His glory. — Psalm 97:5-6

Then the Philistines took the ark of God and brought it from Ebenezer to Ashdod. When the Philistines took the ark of God, they brought it into the temple of Dagon and set it by Dagon. And when the people of Ashdod arose early in the morning, there was Dagon, fallen on its face to the earth before the ark of the Lord. So they took Dagon and set it in its place again. And when they arose early the next morning, there was Dagon, fallen on its face to the ground before the ark of the Lord. The head of Dagon and both the palms of its hands were broken off on the threshold; only Dagon's torso was left of it. Therefore neither the priests of Dagon nor any who come into Dagon's house tread on the threshold of Dagon in Ashdod to this day. But the hand of the Lord was heavy on the people of Ashdod, and He ravaged them and struck them with hemorrhoids, both Ashdod and its territory. And when the men of Ashdod saw how it was, they said, "The ark of the God of Israel must not remain with us, for His hand is harsh toward us and Dagon our god." — 1 Samuel 5:1-7

There is Provision

Let God arise, let His enemies be scattered; let those also who hate Him flee before Him. As smoke is driven away, so drive them away; As wax melts before the fire, so let the wicked perish at the presence of God. But let the righteous be glad; let them rejoice before God; Yes, let them rejoice exceedingly. Sing to God, sing praises to His name; extol Him who rides on the clouds, by His name YAH, and rejoice before Him. A father of the fatherless, a defender of widows, is God in His holy habitation. God sets the solitary in families; He brings out those who are bound into prosperity; but the rebellious dwell in a dry land. O God,

> *when You went out before Your people, when You marched through the wilderness, selah! The earth shook; The heavens also dropped rain at the presence of God; Sinai itself was moved at the presence of God, the God of Israel. You, O God, sent a plentiful rain, whereby You confirmed Your inheritance, when it was weary. — Psalm 68:1-9*

There is Protection & Deliverance From Harm

> *Oh, how great is Your goodness, which You have laid up for those who fear You, which You have prepared for those who trust in You in the presence of the sons of men! You shall hide them in the secret place of Your presence from the plots of man; You shall keep them secretly in a pavilion from the strife of tongues. — Psalm 31:19-20*

There are two more stories from both Old and New Testaments you should consider. Due to space considerations, I will provide only the references so you can look them up and read them in your own Bible.

The first instance is the story of an alliance of three nations attacking Judah during the reign of Jehoshaphat found in 2 Chronicles 20 as I mentioned back in Chapter 4.

The other is the account of Paul and Silas' arrest and imprisonment in Philippi found in Acts 16:16-40.

The Benefits of Worship

Worship is Part of the Teaching Process

> *Let the word of Christ dwell in you richly in all wisdom, teaching and admonishing one another in psalms and hymns and spiritual songs, singing with grace in your hearts to the Lord.*
>
> *— Colossians 3:16*

Praise Enables Us to Tap Into the Joy of Our Salvation

> *And in that day you will say: "O Lord, I will praise You; though You were angry with me, Your anger is turned away, and You comfort me. Behold, God is my salvation, I will trust and not be afraid; For YAH, the LORD, is my strength and song; He also has become my salvation." Therefore with joy you will draw water From the wells of salvation. — Isaiah 12:1-3*

Worship Increases/Releases God's Anointing Upon Those Who are About to Minister

Worship — at least for a brief time — transformed King Saul:

> *After that you shall come to the hill of God where the Philistine garrison is. And it will happen, when you have come there to the city, that you will meet a group of prophets coming down from the high place with a stringed instrument, a tambourine, a flute, and a harp before them; and they will be prophesying. Then the Spirit of the Lord will come upon you, and you will prophesy with them and be turned into another man. And let it be, when these signs come to you, that you do as the occasion demands; for God is with you. — 1 Samuel 10:5-7*

In 2 Kings 3, when the kings of the Northern and Southern Kingdoms summoned Elisha to prophesy over their alliance in their war against Moab, he calls for a musician to play what we can safely assume was worship music. Afterwards, God's anointing came upon Elisha and he prophesied.

In 1 Chronicles 25, we see how King David set aside certain skilled musicians to play and prophesy using their various instruments.

Worship Builds Our Faith

Praise and worship is an excellent means to bring us into agreement with God and build up our faith because good worship songs are either outright Scripture quotations or communicate essential scriptural Truth. When we sing them, we are "confessing" God's Word over ourselves.

I've already delved into the value of confessing the Word over ourselves in previous chapters, so I won't repeat myself here. But I will say that the power of music when coupled with us hearing ourselves proclaim God's Truth to ourselves is a potent combination whose effectiveness cannot be overstated.

Because we are accompanying God's Truth with music, it is communicating that Truth directly to our hearts, even when:

- Our minds may be in turmoil from FUD (Fear, Uncertainty, Doubt)
- We are angry over our negative circumstances, or sins committed against us
- We are struggling with confusion over who and what we are as human beings and believers
- We are unsure about our future
- We are struggling with the Truth that God is really Who He says He is and He will do for us what He says He will do.

The Sacrifice of Praise

Sometimes, we find ourselves in circumstances where it's a struggle to worship because of:

- We are facing one or more real or perceived disasters
- Our strong negative emotions, such as fear, anger, resentment, envy, and other emotional turmoil
- Emotional pain
- Mental confusion

- Emotional/physical exhaustion.

When such times roll around — and they indeed will, regardless of our spiritual maturity level — our solution is offering the "sacrifice of praise."

> *Therefore by Him let us continually offer the sacrifice of praise to God, that is, the fruit of our lips, giving thanks to His name.*
> *— Hebrews 13:15*

Let's unpack this verse a bit:

offer the sacrifice (*anaphero*)

to keep on placing upon an altar

praise (*ainesis*)

thank offering

fruit of our lips (*karpos cheilos*)

fruit born of our speaking mouth

giving thanks (*homologeo*)

same words

Here's a little more accurate translation:

> *Therefore, by Him, let us always be placing a thank offering upon the altar, the words of our mouths agreeing with Him.*

A sacrifice of praise occurs when we deliberately choose to worship God *while our flesh is screaming out for us to do anything else.*

We can only offer that sacrifice this side of eternity. In heaven, there is no sorrow, no loss, no grief, no travail, no tears, no lack, no illness. We steward such moments by laying all those negative emotions at His feet and exalt Him has the Lord Most High.

I've had opportunity to do this many times. Sometimes, the situation completely turned around. Others? Not so much! But this sacrifice is not about obtaining results, it's about abandonment to His goodness, trusting Him to be the loving, gracious Father He has revealed Himself to be.

What is remarkable is whenever we do offer that sacrifice, His tangible presence often manifests on the scene and calms all those negative things by bringing us His peace. I know this for a certainty by experience.

Conclusion

Why should we praise and worship God?

1. It's a reasonable response to Him for everything He has done for us.
2. Though God is always in and with us as Christ-followers, worship invites God's tangible presence onto the scene. In His presence is:
    - Fullness of joy and pleasures forevermore
    - God's power and provision
    - Protection and deliverance from harm (physical, mental, emotional, spiritual)
3. Worship prepares our hearts to receive from God's Word
4. Worship increases and releases the anointing upon God's ministers so God can use them to teach/comfort us more effectively.
5. It builds and reinforces our faith in God and His Word.
6. Worship is an effective response whenever the circumstances of life are exalting themselves against our relationship with God.

So where's the downside?

Nowhere in sight!

CHAPTER 19

Fasting

NO BOOK ON PRAYER WOULD BE COMPLETE without addressing the spiritual discipline of fasting. The phrase "prayer and fasting" appears throughout the Scriptures, so much so it has passed into popular culture.

What exactly *is* the role of fasting in the prayer life of a believer? And equally important, when and where does our fasting depart from its sound biblical basis and devolve into us performing dead religious works?

I will not delve into this topic in serious depth here. Why? Because more than a few anointed authors have written excellent books on fasting. What I hope to achieve is to inspire you to either incorporate fasting into your prayer life — assuming you haven't already — or take your fasting up a notch. More importantly, I hope to steer you away from several significant pitfalls when engaging in this spiritual discipline.

What is Fasting?

Fasting is a voluntary and temporary abstinence from something which sustains or pleases us. The general principle in play is this: we are choosing to engage with our Heavenly Father about some issue which is far more important to us than the gratification of our earthly desires. In the Scriptures, fasting is almost always focussed on food.

We can abstain from:

- Eating food (entirely, favorite foods, or desserts)
- Drinking water (there is one major physiological limitation in play here: if you try to go without water for more than a couple of days, you can damage your internal organs and/or die — *don't push it!*)
- Drinking alcoholic or other beverages
- Watching television
- Intimate relations with our spouse (again, only for a limited time, though; see 1 Corinthians 7)
- Participating in social media
- Some other hobby we enjoy
- And so on…

A fast can span several hours, one or more days, one or more weeks, or even months — basically as long as you feel led to continue.

Fasting is a form of full-on spiritual warfare, against:

- Our own fleshly desires
- The schemes, works, and intentions of the satanic realm

Fasting = Sacrifice

Fasting is a form of sacrifice to our Heavenly Father. For a sacrifice to be of any value whatsoever, it *must* cost us something.

We find one case-in-point in the Old Testament account of David numbering the people of Israel. We take up this account after the plague had already started. The Lord had spoken through the prophet Gad, commanding David to burn offerings on the threshing floor of a local miller named Araunah so the plague would stop. When David arrived, Araunah offered to give his king everything he needed outright. David responded with:

> *Then the king said to Araunah, "**No, but I will surely buy it from you for a price; nor will I offer burnt offerings to the Lord my God with that which costs me nothing.**"*
>
> *So David bought the threshing floor and the oxen for fifty shekels of silver. And David built there an altar to the Lord, and offered burnt offerings and peace offerings.*
>
> *So the Lord heeded the prayers for the land, and the plague was withdrawn from Israel.*
>
> *— 2 Samuel 24:18-25 (emphasis mine)*

Our faithful Lord *always* honors any sacrifice made with a sincere heart and pure motives. How and when His reward appears is at His discretion, not ours; after all, we work for Him, not the other way around! *But He is always faithful to reward us.* On the other hand, God has no regard for sacrifices offered by rote as a dead religious work.

The greatest sacrifice we can make is found in Romans:

> *I beseech you therefore, brethren, by the mercies of God, that you present your bodies a living sacrifice, holy, acceptable to God, which is your reasonable service. — Romans 12:1*

If our fasting does not flow from that heart of surrender to the Most High, *we achieve nothing.*

When Do We Stop?

I can think of only 4 reasons for ending a fast:

1. We see the answer(s) to our prayers.
2. The Holy Spirit tells us our task is complete.
3. We reach the end of our human endurance.
4. We simply call it a day and quit for whatever reason

The first two render further fasting superfluous. Either we have seen our answer manifested or the Holy Spirit assures us our assignment is over and the answer is on its way.

The third implies there is a physiological reason for calling it a day. Examples could be that we need water so we won't die of thirst, or we have a health condition where long-term abstinence from food is not medically recommended (diabetes is one which comes to mind)

Bad Attitudes & Behavior Can Negate Our Fasts

The longest, most renowned Bible passage on fasting is in Isaiah 58:

> *Cry aloud, spare not; Lift up your voice like a trumpet; Tell My people their transgression, and the house of Jacob their sins. Yet they seek Me daily, and delight to know My ways, as a nation that did righteousness, and did not forsake the ordinance of their God. They ask of Me the ordinances of justice; They take delight in approaching God.*
>
> *"Why have we fasted?" they say, "and You have not seen? Why have we afflicted our souls, and You take no notice?"*

> *In fact, in the day of your fast you find pleasure, and exploit all your laborers. Indeed you fast for strife and debate, and to strike with the fist of wickedness. You will not fast as you do this day, to make your voice heard on high.*
>
> *Is it a fast that I have chosen, a day for a man to afflict his soul? Is it to bow down his head like a bulrush, and to spread out sackcloth and ashes? Would you call this a fast, and an acceptable day to the Lord?*
>
> *Is this not the fast that I have chosen: to loose the bonds of wickedness, to undo the heavy burdens, to let the oppressed go free, and that you break every yoke? Is it not to share your bread with the hungry, and that you bring to your house the poor who are cast out; when you see the naked, that you cover him, and not hide yourself from your own flesh? — Isaiah 58:1-8*

We can easily draw two conclusions from this passage:

1. Isaiah was addressing people who endeavored to seek God, delight in Him, and obey His laws. That's to their credit. But despite all that, they were still not getting their prayers answered despite the fact they were fasting. Their natural response was the equivalent of, *"Hey, God! What's up with this!? We thought we were doing 'the right thing!'"*

2. Those folks had lost sight of the attitude of their hearts. Despite their abstention, they were evidently getting drunk, abusing their employees, engaging in strife, division, and fault-finding, ignoring the poor, and were even physically violent.

I cannot help but see the parallels between this chapter and Jesus' Sermon on the Mount, among other passages in the gospels. God is *far* more interested in the condition of our hearts and our attitude towards others than our outward appearance and dead religious works.

And what does our gracious Heavenly Father promise us if we get our interpersonal acts together and *then* fast?

> *Then your light shall break forth like the morning, your healing shall spring forth speedily, and your righteousness shall go before you; the glory of the Lord shall be your rear guard. Then you shall call, and the Lord will answer;*
>
> *You shall cry, and He will say, "Here I am! If you take away the yoke from your midst, the pointing of the finger, and speaking wickedness, if you extend your soul to the hungry and satisfy the afflicted soul, then your light shall dawn in the darkness, and your darkness shall be as the noonday.*
>
> *The Lord will guide you continually, and satisfy your soul in drought, and strengthen your bones; you shall be like a watered garden, and like a spring of water, whose waters do not fail.*
>
> *Those from among you shall build the old waste places; you shall raise up the foundations of many generations; and you shall be called "The Repairer of the Breach," "The Restorer of Streets to Dwell In. — Isaiah 58:9-12"*

Brothers and sisters, that's a heaping helping of goodness. I don't know about you, but that's I want operating in my own life as well as for you!

What is Our Motivation for Fasting?

This leads us to a fundamental truism about fasting, not to mention any works of service/worship we might perform for the Most High:

> *Our attitudes and behaviors towards our fellow man always trump our religious works. If we do all the right things for the wrong motives or while in strife with — or bitterness towards — other people, it counts for nothing, zip, zilch, nada!*

The Apostle Paul, inspired by the Holy Spirit, articulated the concept far more poetically and fluently than I ever could:

> *If I were to speak with eloquence in earth's many languages, and in the heavenly tongues of angels, yet I didn't express myself with love, my words would be reduced to the hollow sound of nothing more than a clanging cymbal.*
>
> *And if I were to have the gift of prophecy with a profound understanding of God's hidden secrets, and if I possessed unending supernatural knowledge, and if I had the greatest gift of faith that could move mountains, but have never learned to love, then I am nothing.*
>
> *And if I were to be so generous as to give away everything I owned to feed the poor, and to offer my body to be burned as a martyr, without the pure motive of love, I would gain nothing of value. — 1 Corinthians 13:1-3 TPT*

Jesus Himself addressed the issue of motives during the Sermon on the Mount:

> *Moreover, when you fast, do not be like the hypocrites, with a sad countenance. For they disfigure their faces that they may appear to men to be fasting. Assuredly, I say to you, they have their reward. But you, when you fast, anoint your head and wash your face, so that you do not appear to men to be fasting, but to your Father who is in the secret place; and your Father who sees in secret will reward you openly. — Matthew 6:16*

Fasting was never intended for us to appear spiritually fashionable to others — and never has been! Neither is biblical fasting a dead religious work performed within a religious economy.

What do I mean by "a religious economy?"

With the sole exception of biblical Christianity, all world religions and Christianity-based cults throughout history are religious economies. A religious economy occurs whenever folks take the stance of, "If I do this, don't do that, cut this off, grow that out, then God will allow me into heaven and/or bless me somehow and/or not smite me with sickness, poverty, disaster, or death."

This is the faulty premise underlying "give to get," making pilgrimages to holy sites, saying rosaries, etc., *ad infinitum, ad nauseam* (see my article entitled *"Christianity vs. Man's Religion"* linked in this book's Appendix for a much more in-depth exploration of this topic).

Bottom line? *Salvation and blessings by works.*

Tragically, many involved in intercessory prayer fall prey to this trap, proclaiming things like, "I'm gonna fast until something happens!" Many such declarations center on a genuine desire for a major move of God in the earth.

Now is praying and fasting for revival a valuable thing? Is it a praiseworthy motive? Is it indeed scriptural?

You betcha! (see 2 Chronicles 7:14)

But if our underlying motive for fasting is getting God off the dime to fulfill our innermost desires, no matter how ostensibly holy those yearnings may seem, *we are fasting amiss.* This is especially relevant when we are experiencing turmoil and division with our spouses, children, colleagues, church members, political opponents, and non-believers.

Whenever we approach fasting trying to manipulate the Most High, somehow trying to put God in our debt, our fast has degenerated into a religious hunger strike.

Instead, fasting should be the embodiment of our wanting and seeking something we *cannot* see through our temporarily abstinence from something we *can*.

In summary, if we approach fasting with the correct attitude while avoiding the pitfalls I've covered in this chapter, it is an incredibly valuable tool in our prayer toolbox.

CHAPTER

20

A Brief Discussion About Miracles

NO TRUE CHRIST-FOLLOWER HAS PROBLEMS with the Bible's descriptions of God's miracles in the ancient past — we're all in agreement the Word accurately portrays such events, so there is no controversy there at all.

It's only when you talk about God performing miracles in the modern day where you run into problems. You will witness one of two reactions.

1. Those who believe God still does them get really excited.
2. Those who don't get really freaked out.

There is no middle ground — it's a totally polarizing concept!

An interesting point-of-fact in this whole debate is every born-from-above believer on the planet has experienced at least one miracle in his or her life, *without one single exception.*

You might protest my claim, saying, "I've never experienced a miracle!"

Au contraire, you have definitely experienced at least one miracle: Which miracle do I speak of, you may ask?

The New Birth!

When you proclaimed Jesus as Lord of your life and believed in your heart that God raised Him from the dead, The Holy Spirit performed a comprehensive list of actions which are completely miraculous, both in nature and scope:

- He resurrected your spirit from the dead.
- He moved into your physical body, uniting with your spirit and making your physical body His eternal home.
- He cleansed you from all your sins
- He made you the righteousness of God in Christ.
- He translated you from the kingdom of darkness into the kingdom of the Son of His love.
- He seated you with Christ in the heavenlies.
- He inscribed your name in the Lamb's Book of Life
- And the list goes on and on…

What's a Miracle?

A miracle is simply an event where God momentarily suspends the natural laws of time and space in order to accomplish His will in the earth, usually in response to prayer. Since our omnipotent God created those natural laws by speaking them into existence in the first place, He is neither bound nor prevented by them from accomplishing whatever He chooses at any given point in time.

It is also crucial to note how every miracle in the Bible and ever since started with an enormous problem, one which human reasoning, effort, politics, or military action clearly could not resolve favorably.

I find it interesting to note the selfsame folks who vehemently proclaim the absolute sovereignty of God (He can do anything He wants at any time for any reason regardless of what His Word promises us) are almost always the same folks who will vehemently deny He can and does perform modern-day miracles of healing, deliverance, and the like. *Just saying'...*

The widespread refusal to accept the idea God still does miracles is a product of modern and post-modern Western Civilization. Go anywhere in the Majority World where you find Christ-followers and the vast majority of them not only believe in miracles, but indeed experience them. That's because they haven't had the "benefit" of secular-humanist public school systems and theologically liberal seminaries to talk them out of what the Bible clearly states.

The late missionary evangelist T. L. Osborn used to hold crusades throughout Africa, India, Asia, and elsewhere. He would proclaim to crowds of people numbering in the tens and hundreds of thousands how God always confirms His Word with signs following. To wit, *miracles.* He went on to say that if miracles did not happen after he finished preaching, then whatever he said was false and they should not be believe anything he said.

Without fail, God showed up and miracles happened by the hundreds, even thousands. The crippled walked, the blind saw, the deaf heard, the dumb spoke, missing limbs regrew, demoniacs got delivered and set free, all in the wonderful name of Jesus!

Conclusion

Obviously, I am squarely in the camp believing God is still very much in the miracle business. I've experienced far too many of them to believe otherwise. But I'm not here to poke fun at you or put you down if you disagree, nor am I here to persuade you of anything. What I do have to say is this challenge:

What does the Word say?

I dare you study this out in your Bible without relying on the opinions of theologians from any era, simply allowing the Bible to interpret itself. You'll want to employ the hermeneutical standards found in an article I've written entitled *"What Is The Bible & How Do We Interpret What It's Saying?"* linked in the Appendix of this book, allowing the Holy Spirit to reveal Truth to you as you do.

Then draw your own conclusions.

Whether you end up agreeing with me at the end of that study or not, your walk with God will be richer for the experience.

It just might transform your prayer life into something you could never have imagined!

CHAPTER

21

How to Pray When Your Life is on the Line

TEN YEARS AGO ON JUNE 23, 2013, our brother in Christ, Nik Wallenda, established a new world record by being the first man to walk successfully across the Grand Canyon on a tightrope (actually a wire cable) using neither a net nor a safety tether.

My wife and I watched the entire event with an other-worldly combination of incredible suspense and spiritual joy as history was being made by a man who boldly and unashamedly bore public witness to the Living Christ to 13 million worldwide viewers while performing this incredible feat.

One thing which impressed me about Brother Nik is someone has taught him — and taught very well, I might add! — how to pray effectively. As we watched, I thought to myself, "Self, I wish every believer could/would pray the same way. They'd sure get a lot more of their prayers answered!"

The Event Itself

What I want to do in this chapter is have you play the publicly available video footage of Nik's feat on YouTube and then allow me to make some brief comments afterward. Here is a QR code linked to the video so you can view it before moving on with this chapter. Simply use a code scanning app on your mobile device or computer to navigate there.

My Comments

There appeared to be no doubt in Nik's mind God would answer his prayers. His trust in the promises of God and the God Who made them was absolute, or he would never have made the attempt.

There was no vagueness in his prayers. Nik specifically asked for — and received — what he wanted from God. There was no "God, please be with me" as so many spiritually flabby, anemic-in-prayer believers pray. Nik knew our Jesus was already in and with him on that wire. God is already "with" — indeed, inside! — every believer, so praying for God to be with us expresses unbelief, not faith.

There was no wishy-washiness in his prayers. You never once heard the Religious Escape Clause, "if it be Your will," come out of his mouth (see Chapter 11). He knew the will of God: he was supposed to complete his walk across without incident while under God's protection — and was operating in agreement with that will.

He also operated on the principles found in Mark 11:22-24 (see Chapter 14) by praying to God, receiving His answer by faith, then speaking to the mountain:

In Nik's case, his mountains were the crosswinds and the oscillating wire upon which he was walking. In his mind and heart, he had already received the answer to his prayer before he ever put one foot on that wire.

Nik worshipped his way across the wire, magnifying God rather than his obstacles. He exuded the confidence which comes from intimately knowing his God as well as knowing and believing the Word — he had totally confidence God had him safely in the palms of His hands.

He paused whenever he needed to, rather than foolishly forging ahead, regardless. Frequently, those who are spiritually immature will throw out reason, experience, and wisdom, deluding themselves into thinking they are thus demonstrating their "great faith." Nik relied not only on God's protection and answers to his prayers, but there were also moments when he paused and "took a knee" on the wire to dampen its oscillations as his own experience dictated.

Conclusion

Unfortunately, a full-length video of this event is not available online, but if you could see it in its entirety, you would see the above characteristics demonstrated all the way across the canyon. It is a marvel to me how the secular Discovery channel didn't edit out the spiritual aspects of this feat, though I imagine that could have been part of Nik's negotiations with them beforehand.

Since that momentous occasion, Nik has performed similar feats, the most recent instance I can recall being his walking a wire strung across the active Masaya volcano just outside Managua, Nicaragua. All the way across, he was singing one of our favorite worship songs. *Raise a Hallelujah* by Bethel Music. The man is no singer, but he definitely makes a joyful noise!

In closing, though I'm no apologist for the man, I would like to address all those folks who love to take cheap shots at Joel Osteen. Joel and his wife were present on-site for the Grand Canyon event — evidently Nik is either one of their congregants or a friend — and they prayed for him prior to the attempt.

It was an equally faith-fill prayer!

CHAPTER

22

The Whole Armor of God

I CANNOT EVEN BEGIN TO COUNT the number of sermons, books, and other teachings I've encountered on this topic over the last 50 years and counting.

As I was listening to my wife cite the latest version from a best-selling Christian author's book, it suddenly hit me: in every instance I can remember, the authors — while excellent teachers all — displayed a distinct lack of knowledge concerning actual ancient warfare when soldiers were wearing armor and wielding swords and shields. While some had presented accurate descriptions of the equipment, no one I have ever heard or read had accurately portrayed how they were actually used in combat!

Another aspect of such teachings is how those teachers focused entirely on the function of each piece of armor individually, but rarely — if ever — describe how those pieces work together while fighting.

Let's explore how introducing that kind of information impacts this teaching and then apply the results to our prayer lives.

The Foundational Scriptures

We find the passage for this teaching in the sixth chapter of Paul's Epistle to the Church at Ephesus:

> *Finally, my brethren, be strong in the Lord and in the power of His might. Put on the whole armor of God, that you may be able to stand against the wiles of the devil, for we do not wrestle against flesh and blood, but against principalities, against powers, against the rulers of the darkness of this age, against spiritual hosts of wickedness in the heavenly places.*
>
> *Therefore, take up the whole armor of God, that you may be able to withstand in the evil day, and having done all, to stand. Stand therefore, having girded your waist with truth, having put on the breastplate of righteousness, and having shod your feet with the preparation of the gospel of peace; above all, taking the shield of faith with which you will be able to quench all the fiery darts of the wicked one and take the helmet of salvation, and the sword of the Spirit, which is the word of God; praying always with all prayer and supplication in the Spirit, being watchful to this end with all perseverance and supplication for all the saints*
> *— Ephesians 6:10-18*

Re-enactor dressed as a Roman infantryman

Since Paul was a Roman citizen and Roman soldiers were ubiquitous throughout the empire, it is almost certain the armor and weaponry Paul visualized as he was writing this passage were those in use by the Roman army and their auxiliaries of the day, so we will examine each piece of armor using that as a logical assumption.

Swords

Every Bible teacher I've ever heard or read makes the erroneous claim we use a shield and armor only for defense and a sword only for offense.

Sword Misconception #1

As someone who has become relatively skilled in two different forms of sword combat (European épée fencing and Japanese *kenjutsu*), I can handily refute such teaching through a simple demonstration in a matter of minutes. Neither sport fencing (all three styles of which hearken back to actual European swordplay) nor *kenjutsu/kendo* rely on the presence of a shield, yet practitioners skilled in those arts can defend themselves quite nicely without one, thank you very much! These are only two examples of sword combat requiring no shield for defense — there are many more!

In our keynote passage for this chapter, Paul used the Greek word *machaira* for "sword":

machaira

a small straight sword used for thrusting/stabbing

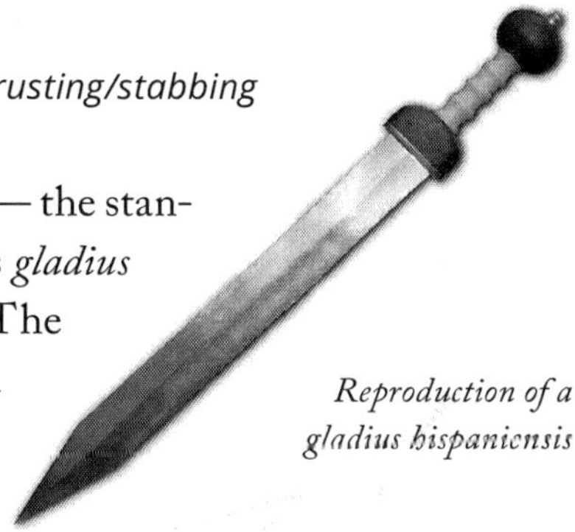

Reproduction of a gladius hispaniensis

The Latin term for just such a sword — the standard Roman sidearm of the day — is *gladius hispaniensis*, or "Spanish sword." The word *gladius* is where we get our term for a class of person who wielded one professionally: a gladiator.

The double-edged blade of a gladius was about 24-inches long and sharpened to a needle point which could easily punch through the inferior chain-mail and leather armor used by many of the Roman army's barbarian opponents.

Defense With A Sword

So how do you defend yourself from an attack using nothing but your own sword?

By parrying!

A parry takes place whenever you use your blade to block or redirect your opponent's attack so it doesn't hit you. You then follow this up with a *riposte* (counterattack).

We fencers call a sequence of such actions (attack-parry-riposte, etc.) a "phrase." When in combat, you string a series of such phrases together until either you or your opponent lands an attack and scores. In modern sport fencing or *kendo*, that's merely a point displayed on a scoreboard. In ancient times, landing an attack resulted in one of the following physical wounds:

1. A scratch or shallow cut
2. A non-fatal penetrating wound or deep cut into/through muscle/fat tissue, but severing no major blood vessels
3. A fatally severed major blood vessel, such as the carotid or femoral arteries
4. A fatal penetrating wound to vital organs, such as the heart, liver, or GI tract
5. Losing a limb, most likely fatal due #3 above
6. Decapitation

Unlike European-style duels which often ended when one duelist drew first blood, a shallow cut doesn't end it in pitched battles — only a fatal or incapacitating wound to your opponent will suffice because he otherwise may continue/resume his attack on you or your fellow soldiers after you have moved on to another opponent. Both the movies *Gladiator* and *Braveheart* portray this kind of horrific combat pretty accurately.

When wielding the Sword of the Spirit, you both attack and defend against the powers of darkness (never fellow human beings — remember, we're not warring not against flesh and blood!).

Sword Misconception #2

Another salient point is your physical Bible is not your sword nor is your pocket Bible your "dagger" nor is the Bible app on your smartphone, tablet, or computer your "light saber."

Here's why: the Greek word translated as "Word" in "Word of God" in this passage is not *logos* (the written Word of God), but *rhema*, the spoken Word of God. Here's the difference:

logos

> *the sayings of God; a decree, mandate or order of the moral precepts given by God; Old Testament prophecy given by the prophets*

rhema

> *that which is or has been uttered by the living voice*

We wield the sword of the Spirit whenever we *speak* the Word, not when we read, study, memorize, or think about it. This is further borne out in passages where John describes his vision of Jesus in the Book of Revelation.

> *Then I turned to see the voice that spoke with me. And having turned I saw seven golden lampstands, and in the midst of the seven lampstands One like the Son of Man, clothed with a*

> *garment down to the feet and girded about the chest with a golden band. His head and hair were white like wool, as white as snow, and His eyes like a flame of fire; His feet were like fine brass, as if refined in a furnace, and His voice as the sound of many waters; He had in His right hand seven stars,* ***out of His mouth went a sharp two-edged sword,*** *and His countenance was like the sun shining in its strength. — Revelation 1:12-16 (emphasis mine)*

> *Now I saw heaven opened, and behold, a white horse. And He who sat on him was called Faithful and True, and in righteousness He judges and makes war. His eyes were like a flame of fire, and on His head were many crowns. He had a name written that no one knew except Himself. He was clothed with a robe dipped in blood, and His name is called The Word of God. And the armies in heaven, clothed in fine linen, white and clean, followed Him on white horses. Now* ***out of His mouth goes a sharp sword,*** *that with it He should strike the nations. And He Himself will rule them with a rod of iron. He Himself treads the winepress of the fierceness and wrath of Almighty God. And He has on His robe and on His thigh a name written: KING OF KINGS AND LORD OF LORDS. — Revelation 19:11-16 (emphasis mine)*

Reproduction of a Roman scutum. The markings on this example indicate its owner is a member of the 30th Legion

Shields

The Greek word for "shield" is *thureos*:

thureos

a large oblong, four-cornered shield

This directly corresponds to a Roman *scutum*, their standard-issue shield.

A *scutum* was rectangular in shape, deeply curved along the vertical axis, and constructed of three layers of wood glued together (an ancient version of plywood), covered in canvas or leather, and bound on all sides with a metal rim, with a large *umbo* (domed steel plate) riveted at its center. This resulted in a well-built and extremely sturdy shield. Dimensionally, it was about ¼-inch thick, stood about 42-inches tall, had an effective width of about 26-inches, and weighed about 22 pounds. The decorations on the front indicated which legion the shield's owner was assigned to.

The shape and size of the *scutum* allowed packed formations of legionaries to overlap/interlock their shields to provide an effective barrier against missiles (darts, arrows, javelins, rocks, etc.).

Re-enactors performing a testudo formation

The most novel (and specialized, for it afforded negligible protection against other attacks) use of the *scutum* was the *testudo* (Latin for "tortoise") formation in which the first rank of legionaries held their shields vertically and interlocked, with the subsequent ranks holding their interlocked shields over their heads to protect against descending missiles, such as arrows or objects thrown by defenders from walls.

The Shield Misconception

The typical sermon on the armor of God would describe a shield as purely defensive, but in actual use, a shield is also a weapon in its own right. Here are some examples of its use as an offensive weapon:

Shield Bash: This is a forward-movement attack where you use your shield as a battering ram by running/lunging at your opponent and slamming into him with it. This is the very reason a *scutum* had a steel *umbo* in its center.

Shield Swipe: This is executed when you swing it at your opponent from one side to the other, knocking both his weapon and defenses aside and then simultaneously following that up with an attack using your sword to stab or slash at a whatever vulnerable targets become available.

Foot Slam: Another tactic unique to shields like the Roman *scutum* was to slam the bottom edge down onto your opponent's foot — probably breaking it — thereby distracting him with the pain, crippling his ability to move, as well as temporarily pinning him in place for you to stab and slash at while he was simultaneously trying to defend himself and recover.

In the hands of a soldier trained in the proper use of both together, a sword and shield are a potent combination for both attacking your opponent and keeping his counterattacks at bay. But what happens when your active defenses fail?

That's what armor is for!

The Rest of the Armor

If you could perfectly defend yourself using only a sword and shield 100% of the time against one or more opponents regardless of their numbers, size, skill, or strength, body armor would be necessary. Indeed, it would be detrimental because such armor adds weight and hinders movement.

But, as an imperfect human being facing someone who might be stronger, quicker, more agile, and/or more skilled — or worse still, facing multiple opponents — having some backup protection is a mighty handy thing to have on your body.

While armor is indeed totally defensive, you can wield items of armor attached to your limbs offensively as well. You can use both *manica* (arm guards) and *greaves* (shin guards) to strike your opponent and *caligae* (boots) to kick or stomp him.

But other than those very limited exceptions, armor comprises a "passive defense." What I mean by "passive" is the soldier *wears* them, rather than *wields* them. Armor exists for the sole purpose of protecting you when your active defenses (sword and shield) fail to protect you.

Your boots are necessary to endure the hardships of long forced marches, though as we just covered, kicking and stomping with them are certainly valid uses.

The Breastplate

Most American preachers wildly misunderstand breastplates. In modern times, we associate the term "breast" with the front half of the human torso. Therefore, many mistakenly assume a breastplate is armor which only covers the front of your body.

Not so!

The Greek word for "breastplate" is *thorax*, which means:

thorax

> *the breast, the part of the body from the neck to the navel, where the ribs end;*
>
> *a breastplate or corset consisting of*

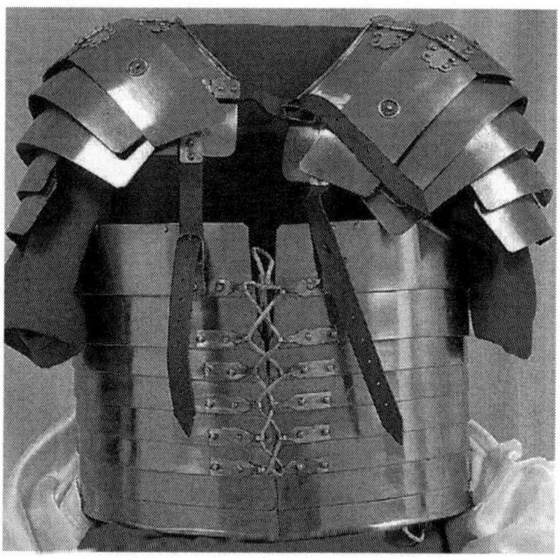

Reproduction of a lorica segmentata

> *two parts and protecting the body on both sides from the neck to the middle*

The first definition of this Greek word is what we use in modern parlance to describe a region of the human body. But the second definition far more accurately defines the type of armor Roman soldiers actually wore.

Their version of such armor was the *lorica segmentata*, or "segmented armor," comprised a series of articulated bands of steel covering both sides of the torso and the shoulders. This was far more effective — especially more puncture resistant — than the typical chain-mail or leather armor worn by their opponents of the day. The segmentation allowed reasonably good freedom of movement while still affording superior protection to barbarian counterparts.

The Helmet

Helmets are the least misunderstood piece of armor because they are still in daily use in modern times by both military personnel and civilians, the chief civilian application being to protect the heads of cyclists, racing drivers, and football/baseball/hockey/etc. players as they engage in their respective sports.

Reproduction of a Roman galea. The sideways crest indicates its owner is a centurion, the commander of 100 men.

The Roman helmet or *galea* was typically constructed of steel, often with brass decorations. High-ranking officers, such as generals and tribunes, would have helmets trimmed in gold instead of brass. They had:

- A short bill affording both a modicum of protection of the eyes from the sun, but also deflected downward slashes to the face

- Small extensions on each side protecting the ears
- A neck guard similar to modern firefighters' helmets
- Hinged cheek-pieces protecting both sides of the face, with a leather thong tied under the chin to hold the helmet on the head
- A socket on top into which they could insert a crest made of dyed horsehair or feathers. The size, shape, color, and orientation (front-to-rear or sideways) indicated the rank of the wearer.

Boots

Ask any modern-day infantryman or marine and he will be the first to affirm the fact proper footwear is a critical component to any soldier's existence — it not only protects his feet during troop movements and combat. Boots are also weapons which can be wielded to kick or stomp your opponent during hand-to-hand combat.

Reproduction of Roman caligae

Caligae were the Romans' answer to this need. Though caligae were constructed of 3 plies of tough leather with hobnails on the bottom for reinforcement and traction, they were what we in modern times call "sandals." Soldiers normally wore their *caligae* over bare feet, but whenever they encountered snowy terrain or cold climates, they would don woolen socks under them.

While there were some obvious downsides to wearing sandals in combat, *caligae* were actually healthier for soldiers of the day — an era when medical knowledge of bacteria, viruses, and fungi was still centuries in the future — because they prevented many of the foot problems faced by soldiers wearing closed footwear in later times, such as trench foot, athlete's foot, and infected blisters.

Putting it All Together Spiritually

Sword & Shield

Just as a Roman legionary wielded a physical gladius and scutum as inseparable partners in both the attack and the defense, so too the spoken Word of God and our faith are equally inseparable in our battles against the negative circumstances in our lives and the powers of darkness.

Our faith is in the character, will, and ability of the One True God as revealed in His Word. When we speak the promises of God's Word in prayer, it carries the same power as when He spoke the universe into existence. His spoken Word is a creative force resounding through the spirit realm, calling angels to attention and obedience to perform God's will as it comes from our lips. His spoken Word stabs and slashes the devil and his legions arrayed against His Church, causing them to abandon their evil schemes and retreat, shrieking with fear and pain. Jesus Himself said the victory is ours and the gates of Hell cannot stand against us!

Speaking of the Body of Christ...

We are supposed to be standing shoulder-to-shoulder with one another, interlocking our shields and wielding our swords as one, having one another's backs, mercifully and compassionately protecting and caring for our wounded (rather than turning on and attacking them as so many religious folk are tragically prone to do), operating in the unity of our faith at the direction of the Holy Spirit. Just as the interlocked shields of the Roman legions protected the entire unit, so too our interlocked faith protects not only our own persons but also our families and our brothers and sisters in Christ, as well.

The Rest of the Armor

What happens when an attack sneaks past our sword and shield? Our passive armor takes over as our protection! The imparted righteousness of Jesus protects our heart and innermost being:

> *For He (God) made Him (Jesus) who knew no sin to be sin for us, that we might become the righteousness of God in Him.*
>
> *— 2 Corinthians 5:21 (parentheses mine)*

When Daddy God looks upon us, He doesn't see us as the colossal screw-ups we tend to be, but as sinless, holy, blameless, spotless and without blemish, washed in the precious blood of His beloved Son. *We need to see ourselves the same way.*

The helmets we wear, our assurance of salvation, protect our thoughts from fear of rejection by God when we fail. Our salvation is by grace alone through faith alone in Christ alone, not on our performance or lack thereof. Such knowledge gives us confidence nothing will separate us from the love of God, that we are accepted in the beloved.

Our loins are girded with God's Truth, further protecting our innermost parts. While we may receive wounds from life's circumstances, nothing can touch the core of our being or shake us out of our confidence in God's Truth: the goodness of God as well as the totality of our salvation and the righteousness which was imparted to us upon conversion.

What are we standing on? The peace which comes from our confidence in the Good News of God's Kingdom manifesting through His sons and daughters on this earth, that we are inseparable citizens of that kingdom, and God's *shalom* which surpasses all human comprehension is guarding our hearts and minds in Christ Jesus.

Man, I just preached myself excited! I'm fired up to go out and kick some devil heinie! *You coming?*

CHAPTER

23

The Warrior Ethos

WE'VE ALL HEARD SERMONS REFERRING to the Body of Christ as "the Army of the Lord" and we've just finished discussing the spiritual armor we have available to us. Many of us have also sung hymns echoing such sentiments, such as my childhood favorite, *Onward, Christian Soldiers.* William Booth thought so highly of the concept he named his organization the "Salvation Army."

> *"Yet I considered it necessary to send to you Epaphroditus, my brother, fellow worker, and fellow soldier, but your messenger and the one who ministered to my need;" — Philippians 2:25*

> *You therefore must endure hardship as a good soldier of Jesus Christ. No one engaged in warfare entangles himself with the affairs of this life, that he may please him who enlisted him as a soldier. — 2 Timothy 2:3-4*

The problem is that most believers have never served in the military at all, much less in combat, so have little or no frame of reference as to what is involved. Most people assume being in the military means having really short haircuts, wearing uniforms, marching in formation, mindlessly obeying orders, training to kill people with various weapons, and during times of war, actually killing them and hopefully coming back in one piece physically and mentally.

<LOUD BUZZER> Sorry, wrong answer! Thank you for playing!

In this chapter, we're going to explore what motivates warriors in combat. Cases in point:

- What does it take for a soldier or marine to Charlie Mike (Continue the Mission) when his brothers-in-arms — often his closest friends, the very people to whom he entrusts his very life — are falling like flies around him, maybe even dying in his arms, with machine-gun bullets and artillery shrapnel buzzing a few inches over his head, and whatever is next seems impossible to accomplish?
- What causes a naval crewman such as my step-father to remain at his battle station, performing his engine-room duties completely unseen deep in the bowels of the ship while his ship is getting pounded into scrap metal by enemy shell-fire and/or aircraft attack?
- What motivates pilots to press home attacks on vital, heavily defended targets while the enemy fills the sky with triple-A (Anti-Aircraft Artillery) and SAMs so thick it feels like you could step out of the plane and walk on them?
- What motivated General Chesty Puller to proclaim to his marines after ascertaining the Chinese People's Liberation Army had surrounded them at Chosin Reservoir during the Korean War, *"They are in front of us, behind us, and we are flanked on both sides by an enemy outnumbering us 29-to-1. They can't get*

away from us now!" before breaking through the Chinese lines and conducting a valiant fighting retreat to the sea for recovery?

- Or a bit closer to home, what drives a firefighter to plunge selflessly into a blazing building to save the life of a victim or fellow firefighter? Or a police officer to draw his gun and enter a building to stop a madman during a mass shooting?

In other words, what causes otherwise sane men to perform seemingly insane acts of incredible valor, such as charging heavily defended enemy bunkers with only a hand grenade, knowing it's suicidal, continuing forward even after being wounded more than once, often fatally, to win the day?

Though I have served in the US Army, it was never in a war zone because the government was winding down our presence in Vietnam at that time. I cannot begin to fathom such a mind-set from my personal experience.

But I have had the rare privilege of hanging with a few true warriors, one being my aforementioned late step-father who served on a destroyer which fought valiantly enough during WWII in the Pacific to earn a Presidential Unit Citation at the Battle of Santa Cruz. Another is a close acquaintance of mine from church, a former Army Ranger sniper who was made a paraplegic by an IED in Iraq. Yet another is a retired Army general who spent most of his career as a special-ops chopper pilot.

They know I'm grateful for their service, but like most heroes, they would also find the depth of my personal respect and admiration for them awkward and embarrassing, so I generally keep quiet about it.

What is the Warrior Ethos?

Before we can define that, we first need to define both what a warrior and an ethos are — the definitions may not be what came to your mind when I first mentioned them here. We'll take the easy one first:

ethos

> *The characteristic spirit of a community as revealed in its beliefs and aspirations*

Clearly and succinctly defining the term "warrior," however, is extraordinarily elusive. Numerous philosophers have spent plenty of hours and countless words over the centuries trying to formulate such a definition. Here's my best shot:

warrior

> *Being a warrior is a calling above and beyond that of a soldier, someone not only capable of engaging in combat, but who deeply appreciates the importance and measure of that action.*
>
> *The consummate warrior is defined by his indomitable spirit, fierce will, personal integrity, and a willing, vigorous dedication to whatever written or implied code(s) of conduct his government and/or unit might place upon him in addition to his exceptional skill at arms. Special ops communities, such as Navy SEALs, Marine Force Recon, Army Rangers and Green Berets, or the British SAS collectively personify this calling, though there are warriors scattered throughout every armed service in other military occupations.*

Predictably, there is a scarcity of warriors in the Chairborne Brigade at the Pentagon.

That rarity of true warriors in any force is not a recent phenomenon.

> *"Of every 100 men, 10 shouldn't even be there. 80 are nothing but targets, 9 are real fighters. We are lucky to have them, they make the battle. Ah, but one, one of them is a Warrior — he will bring the others back!" — Heraclitus, Greek philosopher ca. 500 BC*

Add the two terms together and this is what you get:

warrior ethos

> *The characteristic spirit of the community of people who are called to be warriors as revealed in their beliefs and aspirations*

The Warrior Ethos Defined

Here is what the community of US military warriors believe and aspire to:

1. I will always place the mission first.
2. I will never accept defeat.
3. I will never quit.
4. I will never leave a fallen comrade.

Now let's explore how these 4 principles apply to the Army of God.

1. I Will Always Place the Mission First

Just what is our mission? Trust me, it's precisely the opposite of what immediately comes to mind whenever we hear the term "goal oriented."

Loving Relationships

Loving God

> *"Jesus said to him, 'You shall love the LORD your God with all your heart, with all your soul, and with all your mind.'"*
>
> *— Matthew 22:37*

Loving One Another

> *"A new commandment I give to you, that you love one another; as I have loved you, that you also love one another. By this all will know that you are My disciples, if you have love for one another." —John 13:34–35*

> *"This is My commandment, that you love one another as I have loved you." — John 15:12*

> *"And walk in love, as Christ also has loved us and given Himself for us, an offering and a sacrifice to God for a sweet-smelling aroma." — Ephesians 5:2*

Loving Our Enemies

> *"You have heard that it was said, 'You shall love your neighbor and hate your enemy.' But I say to you, love your enemies, bless those who curse you, do good to those who hate you, and pray for those who spitefully use you and persecute you…" — Matthew 5:43-44*

Winning the Lost

> *"And Jesus came and spoke to them, saying, 'All authority has been given to Me in heaven and on earth. Go therefore and make disciples of all the nations, baptizing them in the name of the Father and of the Son and of the Holy Spirit, teaching them to observe all things that I have commanded you; and lo, I am with you always, even to the end of the age.'" — Matthew 28:18-20*

Allowing God to Build Us Up Together in Unity

> *Coming to Him as to a living stone, rejected indeed by men, but chosen by God and precious, you also, as living stones, are being built up a spiritual house, a holy priesthood, to offer up spiritual sacrifices acceptable to God through Jesus Christ. — 1 Peter 2:4-5*

Prayer

Prayerlessness — a pandemic in American and European churches — is crippling our ability to accomplish the Church's mission. I wrote this book to help correct that problem.

2. I Will Never Accept Defeat

"Behold, I tell you a mystery: We shall not all sleep, but we shall all be changed—in a moment, in the twinkling of an eye, at the last trumpet. For the trumpet will sound, and the dead will be raised incorruptible, and we shall be changed. For this corruptible must put on incorruption, and this mortal must put on immortality. So when this corruptible has put on incorruption, and this mortal has put on immortality, then shall be brought to pass the saying that is written: 'Death is swallowed up in victory.' 'O Death, where is your sting? O Hades, where is your victory?' The sting of death is sin, and the strength of sin is the law. But thanks be to God, who gives us the victory through our Lord Jesus Christ. Therefore, my beloved brethren, be steadfast, immovable, always abounding in the work of the Lord, knowing that your labor is not in vain in the Lord. — 1 Corinthians 15:51-58

"Now thanks be to God who always leads us in triumph in Christ, and through us diffuses the fragrance of His knowledge in every place. For we are to God the fragrance of Christ among those who are being saved and among those who are perishing. To the one we are the aroma of death leading to death, and to the other the aroma of life leading to life...." — 2 Corinthians 2:14-16

"And you, being dead in your trespasses and the uncircumcision of your flesh, He has made alive together with Him, having forgiven you all trespasses, having wiped out the handwriting of requirements that was against us, which was contrary to us. And He has taken it out of the way, having nailed it to the cross. Having disarmed principalities and powers, He made a public spectacle of them, triumphing over them in it." — Colossians 2:13-15

"For whatever is born of God overcomes the world. And this is the victory that has overcome the world — our faith." — 1 John 5:4

Summary

What can we conclude from these verses? First, Jesus has already won the victory through His death & resurrection. Second, because we are in Him, we inherit that victory. Ergo, *the only way we can lose is if we quit.* We'll deal with that next.

3. I Will Never Quit

> *"Therefore, since we have this ministry, as we have received mercy, we do not lose heart." — 2 Corinthians 4:1*
>
> *"Therefore we do not lose heart. Even though our outward man is perishing, yet the inward man is being renewed day by day. For our light affliction, which is but for a moment, is working for us a far more exceeding and eternal weight of glory, while we do not look at the things which are seen, but at the things which are not seen. For the things which are seen are temporary, but the things which are not seen are eternal." — 2 Corinthians 4:16-18*
>
> *Do not be deceived, God is not mocked; for whatever a man sows, that he will also reap. For he who sows to his flesh will of the flesh reap corruption, but he who sows to the Spirit will of the Spirit reap everlasting life. And let us not grow weary while doing good, for in due season we shall reap if we do not lose heart. Therefore, as we have opportunity, let us do good to all, especially to those who are of the household of faith. — Galatians 6:7-10*
>
> *Therefore we also, since we are surrounded by so great a cloud of witnesses, let us lay aside every weight, and the sin which so easily ensnares us, and let us run with endurance the race that is set before us, looking unto Jesus, the Author and Finisher of our faith, who for the joy that was set before Him endured the cross, despising the shame, and has sat down at the right hand of the throne of God. For consider Him who endured such hos-*

tility from sinners against Himself, lest you become weary and discouraged in your souls. — Hebrews 12:1-3

Summary

If we were invulnerable to being discouraged and presented with the temptation to quit, God wouldn't have given us all these admonitions to beware of it. We are not only warned that discouragement will come, but instructed how to deal with it.

> *"Rejoice in the Lord always. Again I will say, rejoice! Let your gentleness be known to all men. The Lord is at hand. Be anxious for nothing, but in everything by prayer and supplication, with thanksgiving, let your requests be made known to God; and the peace of God, which surpasses all understanding, will guard your hearts and minds through Christ Jesus. Finally, brethren, whatever things are true, whatever things are noble, whatever things are just, whatever things are pure, whatever things are lovely, whatever things are of good report, if there is any virtue and if there is anything praiseworthy — meditate on these things. The things which you learned and received and heard and saw in me, these do, and the God of peace will be with you." — Philippians 4:4-9*

4. I Will Never Leave a Fallen Comrade

> *"Brethren, if a man is overtaken in any trespass, you who are spiritual restore such a one in a spirit of gentleness, considering yourself lest you also be tempted. Bear one another's burdens, and so fulfill the law of Christ. For if anyone thinks himself to be something, when he is nothing, he deceives himself. But let each one examine his own work, and then he will have rejoicing in himself alone, and not in another. For each one shall bear his own load." — Galatians 6:1-5*

In the King James, verses 2 and 5 use the same English word "burden." Some have pointed to this, claiming the Bible contradicts itself. They are actually two entirely different words in the Greek:

burdens (*baros*)

oppressive heaviness, weight, burden, trouble

load (*phortion*)

a burden or load, which may be either heavy or light

The word for "burden" is what we would call discouragement or depression. The word has the connotation of "a boulder" or a similar overwhelming, crushing object, whereas the word for "load" carries the connotation of "the portion allotted to us," kind of like a backpack. What it boils down to is we are responsible for carrying our own backpacks, but are commanded to help those who are under a boulder.

Then we have the word "restore:"

restore (*katartizo*)

to mend (what has been broken or rent), to repair, to complete, to fit out, equip, put in order, arrange, adjust; ethically: to strengthen, perfect, complete, make one what he ought to be

We're supposed to be helping heal our wounded — not reviling them, gossiping about them, humiliating them, vilifying them on social media, and/or otherwise rejecting them. As we fulfill that divine command, we do so with a spirit of gentleness, never exhibiting the hubris of assuming we have "arrived" and are above temptation.

> *"Confess your trespasses to one another, and pray for one another, that you may be healed. The effective, fervent prayer of a righteous man avails much." —James 5:16*

> *"Now you are the body of Christ, and members individually."*
> *— 1 Corinthians 12:27*

This also means we are to be transparent with one another — no fronts, no walls, what you see is what you get — because none of us is more valuable to God or to the Body than another. When we openly admit, "This is what happened to me, this is what I did, this is what I did wrong, this is what I think I did right, this is where I need help and prayer," we are being transparent, vulnerable.

Our churches are supposed to be spiritual hospitals where we as broken people gather to worship the One Who died to unbreak us and receive the love, grace, and Truth we need to become less broken as well as the training needed to effectively minister love, grace, and Truth to other broken people inside and outside its walls.

Churches should never be social clubs where religious folk gather to pat one another on the back about how holy and righteous they are.

Furthermore, a church service's primary purpose is *never* to evangelize the lost — that's the congregation's job! — because targeting a service at the lost means the believers present are never served the spiritual meat needed for them to do what they are called to do. Reaching out to unbelievers *en masse* is for evangelistic meetings and crusades, but never for a church service.

That's not to say there shouldn't be altar calls during a church service; God has a way of reaching those who have gone astray or who haven't experienced the New Birth because the Word empowered by the Holy Spirit can reach anyone at any time, regardless of what is being preached or taught. I'm simply opposed to so-called seeker-sensitive churches dumbing down the message for unbelieving ears, rather than teaching and edifying the Church.

The Body of Christ is the primary means God uses to transmit His grace to us, something church folk tend to forget on a depressingly regular basis. For some reason, God has chosen the same mechanism which damages us — our relationships with other human beings — to also heal us. We are all part of one another, all interconnected, with each of us having a part to play in the lives of one another. When one of us is hurting, all of us should be hurting.

> *"Therefore be merciful, just as your Father also is merciful. Judge not, and you shall not be judged. Condemn not, and you shall not be condemned. Forgive, and you will be forgiven. Give, and it will be given to you: good measure, pressed down, shaken together, and running over will be put into your bosom. For with the same measure that you use, it will be measured back to you." — Luke 6:36-38*

God is incredibly picky about who gets to judge us. He has only one acceptable candidate: Himself! He is the only Person who knows the heart and mind of every human being and He takes an dim view of those possessing vastly inferior credentials who try to take over His job.

That would be anyone and everyone else, including you and me!

Many have abused these verses and others like them to deflect the input of others who would call them into account for their sinful words and deeds. But God doesn't mean we are above criticism and others cannot speak correction into our lives. What He means is we are not allowed to determine someone as being somehow "less than" based upon our take on that person's words and actions, nor are we to abuse someone based upon their perceived faults— or using any other excuse, for that matter!

Conclusion

On the following page you will find a poem written by my friend and former martial arts instructor, Sensei Brannon Bain, which I believe will inspire you. Substitute the word "believer" for "warrior" in that poem and you will begin to really "get" what this chapter is all about! This should be the Church's ethos as we fight on until our beloved Savior's imminent return. *Charlie Mike, Church!*

Last Song of the Warrior

I am a warrior.
The cause for which I fight is true and just.
I stand in the path of my enemy,
Against the harm that would come to those I protect.
I shall not waver
As a stone against the torrent of a great river,
Which flows with the blood of those who have fallen.
Enemies, compatriots, and friends.

I am a warrior.
The cause for which I fight is true and just.
Though there are those that would condemn me,
That I would take the life of my enemy to save that of another,
I shall not waver.
I do not regret the strength of my convictions.
I regret only that my enemy is equally as strong in his.
And so, I stand in the river.

I am a warrior.
The cause for which I fight is true and just.
When the time comes that the river should consume me,
That my blood shall join and flow with those who have come before,
I shall not waver.
For then another shall rise up and take my place,
To bar the path of the enemy, and fight for the cause.
Thus, the river, and the stone, go on.

I am a warrior.
The cause for which I fight is true and just.
I shall not waver.

CHAPTER

24

Know Your Weapons

AS I MENTIONED IN CHAPTER 18, God has taught me several spiritual lessons through animals. Here's another such instance. This time we will discuss the two times I have been attacked by large dogs.

Dog Attack #1

Back when I was 7 years old, my parents and I took a memorable road trip in a 1960 Chevy Corvair sedan from my hometown of El Paso, Texas to Northern California and Southwestern Oregon.

First, we visited my half-sister and her family in Oakland, California. Then we drove up historic US Highway 101 through the redwoods to visit my Aunt Ruth, in Port Orford, Oregon, a small coastal town just north of the mouth of the Rogue River.

Port Orford, the town for which they named a cedar tree species, was officially founded in 1856 and for decades served as a receiving port for mercantile and fishing and a shipping port for the timber industry. The local historical landmark, Battle Rock, is the site of a battle between the first Caucasian settlers and the local Native American tribe in 1851.

Aunt Ruth's house was on a hillside with an enormous picture window through which you could see a gorgeous vista of Battle Rock and the ocean. Upon our arrival, we met up with her just before the close of business at the bank where she worked and then convoyed over to her house.

Upon exiting her car, she went around to the back of the house, intending to come to the front door from inside, unlock it, and allow us to enter. In my childish enthusiasm to be there, I chased after her to the rear door and opened it.

With no warning, her collie watchdog leapt at me out of the darkness and bit me in the face!

I ran around front with blood and tears streaming down my face, screaming in terror. My parents and Aunt Ruth quickly sorted out what happened and hauled me off to nearby Gold Beach to see a doctor.

The dog's upper teeth had hit just below my right eye and the lower ones right at the right corner of my mouth. Since I was still a year away from wearing eyeglasses, that dog came within an inch of me having to wear a pirate's patch over that eye for the rest of my life. The doctor treated me, and like most children, I healed quickly — *at least my body did.*

From that moment onward for the next 11 years, I was absolutely terrified of *all* dogs, regardless of size. Since we only had a cat at home until I was 16 and a 5-pound Yorkshire Terrier from then on, I had no positive experiences with large dogs to mitigate my fear.

Steve, the Attack-Dog Handler

After graduating from high school, one of my very first jobs was as a uniformed rent-a-cop for a security company in Oakland, California. Guess what every guard they hired had to do proficiently?

Handle an attack-trained police dog!

Talk about being tossed into the deep end of the pool for my first swimming lesson! Not only was I dealing with large dogs, but specifically ones trained to bite people on command!

But as I learned what the folks at the company who supplied the dogs taught us, we all discovered to our mutual surprise I had a knack for it as I quickly overcame my terror. In fact, I got to be so good at it, the dog company hired me away from the security company; I worked there until I enlisted in the Army.

During this crash-course in attack-dog handling, I learned an extremely valuable tidbit of information: *how to deal with a dog attack and win.* The details of how to do this are too lengthy for this discussion, but it is entirely safe to say I seriously internalized that lesson!

Dog Attack #2

Fast forward another 7 years to the fall of 1979 when I was back living in El Paso after my honorable discharge from the US Army. I was out taking a walk one evening along Rio Grande Avenue near Lee Street in central El Paso, in the area because my girlfriend-soon-to-be-wife lived nearby.

It was a chilly evening, and I was wearing a quilted-nylon polyfill jacket with my hands in its pockets. Because this isn't a particularly safe neighborhood, I also had a razor-sharp Buck® 110 folding hunting knife in my right hand in the jacket pocket.

As I was walking along the sidewalk, praying and minding my own business, a good-sized German Shepherd took offense at my presence on his turf and launched himself at me out of the darkness from his master's front porch. This dog was not barking to warn me off, but was growling while in a flat-out run with his belly to the ground — he was determined to have a piece of me!

With no conscious thought, in one smooth, continuous move, I immediately drew my knife, opened it, crouched in a balanced stance, and yelled, *"HAH!!!"* at the dog. In that split second, I had instinctively formulated my plan of action, and was prepared to carry it out — I was going to be bitten on the left arm, but that mutt was going to die for the privilege!

To my complete astonishment, the dog did an immediate U-turn and ran back to his porch! The whole incident took place within 20 feet and a couple of seconds.

As you can see, this was an entirely different outcome from the attack when I was 7. In the first instance, I was blind-sided and unable to defend myself. In the second, I defended myself so successfully I didn't even get bitten (Thank You, Jesus!).

The Spiritual Application

Some of you are wondering by now, asking yourselves, "Well, what's the spiritual significance of all this?" A couple of Scripture verses come to mind here:

> *'Therefore my people have gone into captivity, because they have no knowledge…' — Isaiah 5:13a*

> *'My people are destroyed for lack of knowledge…' — Hosea 4:6a*

In both verses, the Hebrew word for "knowledge" is *da'ath*:

knowledge (*da'ath*)

knowledge, perception, skill, discernment, understanding, wisdom

God is saying here His people are destroyed or led into captivity because they lack knowledge, perception, skill, discernment, understanding, and wisdom.

"Knowledge of what?" you may ask.

The context of the verse in Isaiah refers to God's people not regarding, paying attention to, or perceiving His works and purposes in the earth. The context of the verse in Hosea was a mass turning away from God to idols.

In both cases, *the people of God were living their lives with total disregard for their Creator.*

Modern-day church-goers tend to fall into the same kinds of traps, living secular — or even worse: religious — existences oblivious to God's desire to be vitally involved with their daily lives. Some will now nod their heads in agreement, self-righteously affirming how sin is indeed a problem, but unrepented sin is but one facet of this issue.

The far greater tragedy is this: whether through their inaccurate or ineffective revelation of God's Word or a total lack of knowledge about the things of God, they are totally at the nonexistent mercy of Satan, a supernatural psychopath bent on our complete destruction.

Rather than responding to an attack with the expertise and confidence derived from good training (theory + practice + time) in a soldier, such believers either blame the attack on God ("He wants to make me humble" or "He wants me to suffer so I can bring glory to Him", or "He wants to teach me patience," or other pious-sounding religious drivel) or they forget we are not warring with flesh and blood (Ephesians 6:12), start blaming other humans and sinking into bitterness.

Either way, rather than confidently fighting back, they throw down their weapons (assuming they had even picked them up in the first place) and refuse to fight, allowing the enemy to roll over them and/or their loved ones like a tsunami.

When that second dog attacked me, I responded without thinking in accordance with the training I had received. Because I reacted correctly and with total confidence in both my weapon and my knowledge of how to wield it under such circumstances, the attacker was driven off — if it hadn't, the dog would have died right there on the spot. Any way you cut it (pardon the pun), I won the fight!

This book is not theoretical, but practical rubber-meets-the-road applied theology I have experienced in my own walk with God. When I first heard my cancer diagnosis, it never occurred to me to be scared. It was like a cocoon of grace surrounded me and all the years of receiving training in — as well as personally teaching — the Word of God concerning divine healing immediately kicked in. By God's grace — and to His glory! — He had already fully equipped and trained me to face that attack when it came. The end-result is that I am now completely cancer-free for over 10 years and counting.

Conclusion

Over the last two chapters, we've been talking about our spiritual weapons and armor and a warrior's mind-set and ethos. However, neither of them will do us a lick of good if we are untaught and unskilled in how to fight. Becoming proficient with those weapons takes accurate knowledge of the proper principles as well as repeated practice using those principles over time. In other words, having a warrior's spirit and ethos will do us no good whatsoever when we are wielding a knife or club when defending ourselves from an enemy 100 yards away!

Case-in-point: I have a sheathed *wakizashi* (a samurai short sword) standing in the corner of our bedroom at my side of the bed.

- In the hands of my beautiful, intelligent, and godly wife, it is simply a chunk of wood and metal little better than an awkward club.
- In my hands, that selfsame object is a deadly short-range weapon against any intruder.

The difference? *Training!*

No one has ever taught Tess how to fight. In contrast, I've studied *kenjutsu* and other related martial arts. I know the strengths and weaknesses of that sword, the limits of my own skill with it, and how to wield it effectively within those limits.

Countless Christ-followers wait until they have Stage IV cancer before diving into God's Word concerning divine healing. Others wait until they are unemployed and about to become homeless before discovering His promises available to all believers concerning financial provision.

The tragedy is that, while some indeed receive miraculous deliverance from such pickles, the vast majority of them fail.

This is comparable to a Little Leaguer coming up to bat at a major league baseball game at the bottom of the 9th inning with the bases loaded, needing to hit a home run with 2 outs already on the board, and facing Randy "The Big Unit" Johnson on the pitcher's mound — the odds of success are not in that young batter's favor. Not only are the child's skills not up to the task at hand, but the intimidation factor involved in facing such a daunting challenge cannot be understated.

A famous historian once said of the Roman Army:

> *Their drills were like bloodless battles and their battles like bloody drills   The Jewish War by Titus Flavius Josephus, 1st century AD Romano-Jewish historian*

Today's military professionals follow a similar maxim. The harder and better you train in peacetime, the more likely your personal survival as well as achieving victory over your country's enemies.

This is a fundamental truism for every aspect of life.

We get to the same place spiritually by knowing God on a continuously and progressively greater level. As we know Him more closely and intimately, our faith in His Word grows and our skill in handling our weapons and armor increases.

And when that scurvy dog Satan tries to attack us, we respond with "JESUS!!!" and bash him with our shield of faith while cutting him to ribbons with the Sword of the Spirit.

In the words of Paul:

> *We then, as workers together with Him also plead with you not to receive the grace of God in vain. For He says: "In an acceptable time I have heard you, And in the day of salvation I have helped you." Behold, now is the accepted time; behold, now is the day of salvation. — 2 Corinthians 6:1-2*

There is no time like the present to get serious about the things of God, gird your loins with Truth, put on the whole armor of God, and start training with deadly earnest!

Trust me, you will be blessed in the doing of it!

P.S. The next time you train with Deadly Earnest, please give him my fond regards!

CHAPTER

25

Fighting Tooth and Nail

IN CHAPTER 18, I DISCUSSED how God used Tiger, our late orange tabby cat, to teach me about worship. In this chapter, we'll discuss the final lesson He used this precious animal to teach me: *how Tiger died.*

Tiger had been chronically vomiting and shedding weight for a period of months, so we thought he had contracted some sort of disease or condition which elderly cats are prone to develop. We needed to discover what was wrong, whether it was treatable, and should treatment prove impossible or prohibitively expensive, to put him down. So we had the dubious privilege of hauling this little guy to the vet, an event we had never faced together since I took him and his brother to be neutered when they were wee kittens.

He absolutely detested moving scenery and knew the cat carrier's appearance meant precisely that. While it took me two tries to get him in there, fortunately neither of us was worse for wear afterwards. However, once we arrived at the vet and I let him out of the carrier in the vain hope of holding and comforting him until the vet could see him, he got it into his fuzzy little brain his life was in danger.

As a result, he instantly transformed himself from being a fairly docile kitty into a miniature version of his namesake and going full-beast-mode, first hiding under the examining room couch, hissing and growling while steadfastly refusing to come out (the feline equivalent of an extended middle finger), and then going into full-on attack mode when the tech tried to pick him up.

Making a temporary strategic retreat, the tech and vet returned. This time the tech wore a pair of elbow-length heavy leather gauntlets with steel-reinforced fingers.

We've all heard the term I used in the title of this chapter, but few — if any — of us have ever truly witnessed a person or animal doing precisely that. Tiger was doing everything in his earthly power to defend his life in an all-out attempt to dismember/disembowel both the tech and the vet. He fought desperately and valiantly. His battle left his gums bleeding and fang dents in the tech's hands despite those massively heavy gloves. He clawed those gauntlets so murderously, he ripped claws from his own feet, as well as spraining his right-rear leg.

Finally, they restrained him long enough to examine him and draw a blood sample. For you cat lovers out there, it turns out my true worshipper showed zero signs of any diseases or cancer. His blood work did show an abnormally high level of allergic activity. We then had the challenge of determining what he was allergic to and how to mitigate it.

His leg sprain was so severe he could not walk without excruciating pain, so he also had to recover from that injury. Within a day or two, he had recovered enough for me to administer his liquid medication using a syringe with no risk to my person, but he remained an extremely unhappy camper.

Unfortunately, his experience at the vet had psychologically scarred him. Even though he was healthy enough to walk after a couple of days, he steadfastly refused to:

- Come out of whatever hidey-hole he could find
- Eat or drink unless I placed it right in front of him, and even then, hardly at all.
- Use the litter box. He simply eliminated in place wherever he was. Thank God we have tile floors on almost all the ground floor and we could block off the carpeted upstairs with a borrowed toddler gate!

  At one point, he snuck into our bedroom and hid beneath our king-size bed — we had to completely dismantle it to get him out of there so he wouldn't eliminate on the carpet. This event traumatized him even further.

I faithfully medicated him with the steroids the vet had prescribed to deal with the allergies. After a week of Tiger's PTSD behavior, the vet added a tranquilizer to the mix.

The following week passed with zero improvement. His refusal to eat and drink emaciated him far beyond the shadow of his former physique prior to the initial vet visit. Before the initial weight loss started, he weighed a solid 16 pounds — he had shrunk down to half that by the time it was all over.

On what turned out to be his last night in our family, Tiger surprised both my wife and me by jumping up onto my chest while I was watching TV on my recliner. Though his entire hindquarters were soaked with his own urine, I didn't have the heart to push him away, so I pet him on the dry parts of his body until it was time for bed. I then gently placed him on the floor, stood up, washed my clothes, and showered.

It felt like he knew the end was near and was telling me goodbye that night.

The next afternoon, I discussed with my wife what to do with the poor little guy and, after admitting to one another we had seen zero improvement, we reluctantly agreed it was time to pull the plug. I called the vet to schedule euthanasia and cremation, accosted Tiger and doped him to the eyeballs with the tranquilizer/sedative to keep him calm, and transported him to the vet.

He was so soaked in urine, I could not hold him in my arms, so I had to say my goodbye to him through the grill of the cat carrier, then let the tech take him to the back. That was the last I ever saw of him and I could barely keep it together emotionally while dealing with the receptionist to pay the bill.

Tiger was a great kitty, a faithful companion, and an awesome tool of God to teach me the true meaning of worship. As annoying as he could be at times, I still miss him!

RIP, old friend!

Fighting God Tooth and Nail

Looking back on my life, it never ceases to amaze me how I have fought God's dealings with me. Even more amazing is how many people who call themselves Christians do the same thing and beyond.

We are so afraid of the unknown, so terrified of change and what that might bring, so addicted to our comfort zones that whenever God tries to move us away from our utterly selfish ways towards Christ-likeness, we frequently resort to the kinds of emotionally and spiritually combative gymnastics Tiger exhibited at the vet's office. Here's a list, most of which I got from another minister, which I use as a handout in my counseling, support groups, and certain teaching situations:

10 Ways to Run From God

1. **Open Rebellion:** I don't have to accept responsibility for my issues because God has no right to tell me what to do.
    - No, I will not submit!
    - I will not obey!
    - I'll do it my way!
2. **Denial:** I don't have to accept responsibility for my issues because I refuse to acknowledge a problem even exists.
    - That isn't the way it is!<
    - This isn't happening to me!
    - My ___________ isn't really like that!
3. **Excuses:** I don't have to accept responsibility for my issues because of my past or current circumstances.
    - I had a hard day at work
    - My spouse/kids are driving me nuts
    - I was/am abused
    - I was/am poor
    - I don't have ___________.
4. **Blame-shifting:** I don't have to accept responsibility for my issues because of other people's poor choices or bad behavior.
    - If my spouse didn't do ___________, then I wouldn't get angry.
    - If my kids would just stop ___________, then I could get my housework done.

- If my boss would just ___________, then I would be diligent in my job.
- If my husband would just ___________, then I wouldn't get so frustrated with him.

5. **Busy-ness:** I don't have to accept responsibility for my issues because there are too many demands upon my time/attention for me to deal with them.

6. **Procrastination:** I don't have to accept responsibility for my issues because, if I just stall long enough, they will go away.

7. **Walls & Masks:** I don't have to accept responsibility for my issues because I'll hide my true self behind some belief or aspect of my personality where no one can see or touch the core of who I am as a person.

8. **Addictions and/or Codependency:** I don't have to accept responsibility for my issues because I'll compulsively act out in behaviors, substances, or relationships which seem to medicate my pain.

9. **Magical Thinking:** I don't have to accept responsibility for my issues because I will substitute reality with fantasy(ies).
   - If only I could have ___________, my life will be OK.
   - If only I could move to ___________, my life will be OK.
   - If only I could get my parent/boss/spouse/child/significant other to ___________, he/she would ___________ and my life will be OK.

10. **Running (literally):** I don't have to accept responsibility for my issues because I will physically remove myself from the

problem (person, place, or situation) where God is currently dealing with me.

All these are go-to items for those fighting God tooth and nail, especially the second one: *denial.* Denial is the emotional and spiritual equivalent of sticking our fingers in our ears and shouting, "La, la, la, la, la!" to God. This behavior is ultimately what killed Pharaoh (the King of Denial) in the Book of Exodus when he started remembering and re-believing a lie he had lived with his entire life: *I really am a god*!

Oops!

Denial is so pervasive that Step #1 of every 12-step program on the planet is for the addict to abandon his/her denial by admitting they indeed have a problem and their life is out of control. Every time they attend a group meeting, before they can share what is going on in their lives, they announce their name and the phrase, "and I am a recovering alcoholic/addict," again to keep denial at bay.

While all 10 behaviors I've just listed are endemic to a humanity steadfastly resisting the dealings of God in their lives, we usually specialize in one or two of them in our refusal to surrender to the Most High. However, should we persist in any of them long and hard enough, they can prove deadly.

However, God is amazingly patient and gracious.

He is personally eternal, residing outside of space/time, so He can and does allow us to exhaust our stubborn and seemingly endless quests to maintain self-sovereignty over our lives until we "come to ourselves" as the Prodigal Son did aka "hitting rock bottom". He will begin dealing with us in some area of our lives and, when we persist in choosing our own way instead of His, He will allow us to "take another lap around Mt. Sinai" as He did with the children of Israel in the wilderness.

This cycle will continue until we finally surrender and obey.

The penalties for our resistance increase with each and every lap as He keeps raising the stakes until we finally fold.

Poor Tiger fought so hard he physically injured himself, but in the end it was all an exercise in futility. The vet still successfully examined him and drew a blood sample despite his titanic struggles. All Tiger accomplished was to cause himself an incredible amount of physical pain and emotional suffering, ultimately leading to his premature demise. It all could have been avoided had he simply submitted to the entire process peacefully; indeed, it is entirely likely he would have been with me to this day

We have the potential of fighting God so hard and for so long it costs us our lives, not because God takes it from us — that would be theft and only the devil steals from us, kills us, and destroys our stuff (John 10:10) — but because we have so messed ourselves up during the fight, our own rebellion kills us, whether by suicide or some other life-ending situation.

A sobering thought indeed!

Fighting the Devil Tooth & Nail

On another tack, I can't help but wonder what the world — especially our nation — would look like if the Church got off its blessed assurance and fervently prayed, using our God-granted authority over the powers of darkness (see Chapter 6), to go full-beast-mode on the devil with the same level of all-out commitment Tiger showed that day at the vet?

- Would New York and other states have or be passing full-term abortion laws, expanding our nation's genocide of the innocent to include new victims? Would there be abortion-on-demand at all? Would Planned Parenthood still even be in existence?

- Would satanically motivated politicians be in office passing unjust laws to further enslave us?
- Would demonic concepts and behaviors be enshrined in our educational institutions, brainwashing our children with lies from the pit of Hell?

We have an incredible number of passages from God's Word promising we will prevail when we repent and pray, the chief among them being 2 Chronicles 7:14, 1 Timothy 2:1-4, and Hebrews 4:16.

And please don't mistake me for being judgmental here; God is using this very lesson to challenge me to take my own prayer life to the next level!

Selah!

CHAPTER 26

Blessed

ONE OF MY WIFE'S AND MY FAVORITE Bible passages is commonly known as the "Aaronic Blessing," "Aaronic Benediction," or "Priestly Blessing." If you have a religious heritage based in Judaism or a liturgical Christian denomination, such as Presbyterian, Methodist, Episcopalian, or Lutheran, you have certainly heard it pronounced over the congregation by the rabbi or pastor, usually at the end of the service:

> *The Lord said to Moses, "Tell Aaron and his sons, 'This is how you are to bless the Israelites. Say to them:*
>
> *'The Lord bless you and keep you;The Lord make His face shine on you and be gracious to you;The Lord turn His face toward you and give you peace.'*
>
> *So they will put my name on the Israelites, and I will bless them." — Numbers 6:22-27*

In this final chapter, we will unpack this passage and explore just what it means to be blessed by God.

Branding

I want to make my first point from the last verse in this passage:

> *So they will put my name on the Israelites, and I will bless them."*

With this sentence, God is actually branding His people. I'm not referring to the practice of ranchers branding livestock with a red-hot piece of iron here. "Branding" in this sense is a term pervasive in the advertising industry:

branding

> *the promotion of a particular product or company through advertising and distinctive design*

God hand-selected the descendants of Abraham to be His chosen people, the ones designed by Him to distinctively bear His name. They would do that by proclaiming through both word and example the existence, character/characteristics, morality, and goodness of the One True God through their worship and observance of His Law.

The second half of this branding process is the final clause of that sentence: "and I will bless them." Not only would God brand Himself through a people whose behavior would be a light and example for all to see, but He would also bless His people so mightily onlookers would be amazed at their quality of life.

All this would literally advertise The Most High God before a lost and dying humanity wholly given over to idolatry, self-exaltation, and sexual licentiousness.

Christ-followers have since inherited that mantle. We, too, have been branded by our Lord and Savior. However, rather than His Person and message being advertised through our law-keeping, it would instead be characterized by our selfless devotion to Him and self-sacrificing love toward one another and the lost while losing the ethnic trappings/limitations of having to be Jewish.

A quick glance at the quality of social-media discourse proffered by those labelling themselves as Christians these days will quickly show how wretched a job we are doing as His advertisers. But I digress…

The Hebrew Amplification

All this leads us to a crucial question:

How — in what ways — does God bless His chosen ones?

We find our answers when we dig into the Hebrew of this passage, which sounds a lot more like:

May the Lord bless you…

> *May Ha'Shem reach down and make Himself available to you as your Heavenly Father so He can bestow upon you His promises and gifts. May He meet your every need to live successfully on this earth.*

…and keep you…

> *May Ha'Shem guard you with a thorny hedge of protection which will prevent Satan from harming you. May He protect you — body, soul, and spirit — as well as all of your loved ones and earthly possessions. May He also protect you from any moral corruption arising from those possessions.*

The Lord make His face shine upon you…

> *May Ha'Shem illuminate the wholeness of His being toward you, continually bringing you to order so you will fulfill your divine destiny and purpose. May He impart His wisdom to you through enlightenment from His Word.*

...and be gracious to you...

> *May Ha'Shem provide you with His perfect love, intimate friendship, complete forgiveness, showering you with His favor as well as giving you favor with others.*

The Lord lift up His countenance on you...

> *May Ha'Shem turn His head to see you, suppressing any anger towards you, lifting up and conveying the fullness of His Being to you, bringing everything He is and has to your aid, supporting you with His divine embrace.*

...and give you peace (*shalom*).

> *May Ha'Shem set in place all you need to be whole and complete, so you can walk in victory, moment by moment, by the power of His Holy Spirit. May He give you supernatural health, peace, safety, soundness, tranquility, prosperity, perfection, fullness, and harmony as well as the absence of agitation and discord.*

One fascinating aspect of the word *shalom* is its spelling in Hebrew: *shin, lamed, vav, mem*. When you read these pictographs in sequence, they actually form a sentence:

shalom

> *Destroy the authority that binds to chaos.*

When we take into consideration who that authority is — the god of this world, Satan — *shalom* literally destroys his authority to bring and/or imprison us in chaos, confusion, and disarray in any situation!

We can safely conclude the following from all this:

- The One True God commanded — not suggested! — this prayer be prayed specifically word-by-word over His people.
- Therefore, it is His expressed will for *all* His chosen ones, period.

- Since God has grafted all non-Jewish believers into that same tree through saving faith in *Yeshua Ha'Mashiach* aka Jesus the Christ (see Romans 11), we can also safely conclude it is God's will for *all* Christ-followers, period.

Blessings or Suffering?

There are those from certain doctrinal traditions within Christendom — most notably Calvinists — who will dismiss such claims, saying, "But what about all those New Testament verses proclaiming how we are supposed to suffer?"

To which I respond, "This is one of the many tensions, paradoxes, and unfathomable mysteries found in Scripture we will never fully resolve this side of eternity." God has somehow worked it out where we get to be blessed as described above while suffering for righteousness' sake.

I don't know *how* that works, I just know that it *does!*

To see this paradox exemplified in the life of a real-life believer, read Kim Phuc Phan Thi's autobiography, *Fire Road*. Kim is the naked little 9-year-old girl being consumed by napalm as recorded in that 1972 Pulitzer-Prize-winning AP photo on the cover.

Her book poignantly describes her incredible path of suffering over a period of decades while at the same time glorifying our precious Lord Jesus through her vivid descriptions of His salvation, grace, mercy, supernatural provision, and healing power. She describes how He has delivered her from abject poverty, horrendous political oppression, intense personal pain and bitterness, as well as providing the reconciliation, restoration, and salvation of her entire family.

It is an incredible testimony of God's faithfulness to His promises — in many cases, bona fide miracles! — despite overwhelming and seemingly insurmountable odds and obstacles. For what my opinion may matter to you, this book is inspirational, transcendental, and easily one of the best books I've ever read, Christian or non! Several times I was reading it through tears of gratitude to and worship of our Lord.

Blessing Defined

When we look at the definition of the word "blessed" from this passage in the Hebrew lexicon, we find:

bless (*barak*)

to bless

Frankly, this doesn't help our understanding much.

Looking in a modern English dictionary, we find the following among the definitions found there:

bless

to confer or invoke divine favor upon; ask God to look favorably on

We're getting warmer!

We find one New Testament word for "blessed" in Jesus' Sermon on the Mount where He pronounces blessings over certain categories of people. This one, *makarios*, literally means "happy."

While that is cool in and of itself, it still doesn't help us much.

The concept of blessing really comes into focus when we examine another NT word for "bless" and its definition found in the Greek lexicon:

bless (*eulogeo*)

> *to cause to prosper, to make happy, to bestow blessings upon; favored of God; blessed*

Eulogeo literally means "good words." This is where we get our English word "eulogy," a speech given at a funeral which praises the deceased's character and their contributions to family, society, or both.

Remarkably, *eulogeo* is also the selfsame word used by Jesus when He commanded us to:

> *...love your enemies,* ***bless those who curse you,*** *do good to those who hate you, and pray for those who spitefully use you and persecute you — Matthew 5:44 (emphasis mine)*

That is a whole kettle of fish different from the typical so-called Christian discourse on social media and public discussions concerning various doctrines, politics/politicians, media personalities, the education system, and other cultural hot-button issues, now isn't it?

So let's tug on this thread a tad more and see where it leads us:

What happens when God speaks?
Stuff happens! Universes are flung into existence, laws of chemistry, physics, mathematics, and biology are put in place and made effective, stars are born, planets formed, living creatures created (see Genesis 1-2)

What happens when God speaks good things?
Good stuff happens! See the previous list, all of which God called "good."

What happens when God speaks good things over His people?
Good stuff happens to us!

WOW! Pause and *selah* that idea for a bit!

In Closing

I would like to end this book with the following, expressed with the sincere desire you would receive it by faith and make it your own.

This is the will of God concerning you!

> *The Lord bless you, and keep you [protect you, sustain you, and guard you]; The Lord make His face shine upon you [with favor], and be gracious to you [surrounding you with loving-kindness]; The Lord lift up His countenance (face) upon you [with divine approval], and give you peace [a tranquil heart and life].' — Numbers 6:24-26 AMP*

To which I add: *AMEN*!

AUTHOR'S NOTE: I would like to acknowledge and express my heartfelt thanks to my close friend and beloved former Messianic Jewish rabbi, Shmuel Oppenheim, for his invaluable insights on this chapter. He also verified my Hebrew amplification by loaning me his Orthodox Hebrew commentaries. *Shalom, Achi!*

I would also like to note the name of God in the Hebrew used throughout Numbers 6:22-27 is actually *YHWH.* I've substituted *Ha'Shem* (the Name) out of respect for Jewish tradition.

Afterword

WHEN I REFLECT ON MY 7 DECADES on this planet (as of this writing), all I can do is marvel at what God has done. If you've read Chapter 15, you learned a great deal about my childhood and adolescence and what an incredible transformation Jesus has brought about in me. Now, as Paul Harvey used to put it, you'll hear *"the rest of the story..."*

Triple Career Paths

My professional life has had three career tracks, sometimes alternating, other times running concurrently. I started out as an IT guy, doing programming, database design, and system administration. The second tack started in 1985 when I bought my first Macintosh computer. Almost immediately, I was in on the ground-floor of the desktop publishing revolution of the late 1980s and well into the 1990s, creating commercial artwork (books, newsletters, ads, logos, brochures, etc.) for various ministries. All those skills came into play as I designed and typeset this book and its cover, I might add.

I had those two career paths going interchangeably until 1993, when the Internet started being a big deal. Again, I dove into a revolutionary technology in its nascent stage. What had been two separate career paths suddenly married into a third in the design, creation, and coding of websites. Since then, I've been freely swapping back and forth among them as my life progressed.

Prior to my time at my former employer, Life Christian University, my longest tenure with a single company was a 3½ year stint with American Airlines SABRE Computer Services during the early 1990s. Most jobs, though, lasted only a year or so. Some of that, in the early years of my career, was my own doing as I developed a godly work ethic and learned to keep my temper and tongue in check. Everything else was because of circumstances beyond my control. This whole time. I was switching back and forth among my three career tracks.

You can now see why for years, despite my many professional accomplishments, I felt my resume painted me as a failure, like I either couldn't hold a job or figure out what I wanted to be when I grew up.

In 1998, I started my first stint with Life Christian University as their Director of Communications & IT. This position called upon all my skill sets in a single position. After a several-year hiatus for reasons not germane to this story, I returned as their Director of Software Development in early 2010 and remained there until late 2022.

Why the History?

Why is this of any never-mind and why am I inflicting you with all this personal history? The answer lies in two things God spoke into my life, one occurring about a year after my return to LCU and the other on my 60th birthday.

First Instance

Back in late 2009, I had just completed a total redesign/rewrite of some software I had written 10 years prior. The university uses that software to track its student records. That rewrite was a rousing success and everybody at LCU was ecstatic about it. As I entered my office at the university one afternoon, the Lord spoke to my heart and said,

> *"I've been preparing you to accomplish this project for the last 35 years."*

After a brief mental inventory of the skills I had employed to complete the project, ranging from the design of the software's underpinnings and user interface to having written and typeset a professional-quality user manual for the staff, I saw God was, as always, absolutely correct — *its creation leveraged every talent and skill I had developed over the previous 3½ decades.*

At that moment, I ceased to be ashamed of my resume — *God had orchestrated all of it!*

Second Instance

On my 60th birthday as my close friend and former pastor, Ron Merrell, was preaching about worship from Psalm 71, God gave me an awesome birthday present:

> *Now that I am old and gray, do not abandon me O God. Let me proclaim Your power to this new generation, Your miracles to all who come after me. — Psalm 71:18 NLT*

Because we are living under the New Covenant in Jesus' blood, I have no fear of God's abandonment because He promised us He will never leave nor forsake any of us — and God *always* honors His Word!

But I am indeed old and gray and *"Let me proclaim Your power to this new generation, Your miracles to all who come after me"* is indeed the cry of my heart.

That is why I write.

Thank you for honoring the calling of God on my life by reading my scribblings here.

MSW

APPENDIX

In the first edition of this book, some of the opening chapters discussed some key foundational issues, though none of them specifically addressed the subject of prayer. Because each of them was rather lengthy and to make room for the new chapters (all of which are far more directly concerned with the topic at hand), I've replaced those chapters with links to my blog articles on those same topics.

The QR codes below link each article so you can view it in a web browser. Simply use the camera app on your mobile device or computer to navigate to each.

MSW

What Is The Bible &
How Do We Interpret
What It's Saying?

Christianity vs. Man's Religion

Who's in Charge?
The Cosmic Battle for Control

The Prison of Perfectionism

Of Blind Men & Elephants

The God Who Speaks

Double-Minded

The Saints Who Say NIH!

About the Author

MARK STEVENS (STEVE) WILLIS WAS BORN in the desert Southwest, though he has lived in a variety of locales ranging from San Francisco Bay to Tampa Bay and quite a few places in-between over the years.

He has been saved for 50 years as of this edition, has been called to the ministry for most of that time, and was ordained in 2000. Steve earned his Doctor of Ministry degree in 2014 and his PhD in 2019, both in theology. Though he has attended several denominational churches over the years, the bulk of his Christian experience has been in non-denominational charismatic settings.

Besides his writing, he preaches and teaches the Word of God and counsels the abused, the codependent, and the addicted. Steve has served for several years as the leader of an intercessory prayer ministry at a church he formerly attended.

Steve's wife Tess is a Filipina who emigrated to the US to be with him. They now live in the high desert of Northern Arizona. He has a married daughter, a married son, and 3 grandchildren. Tess has a married daughter, an unmarried son, and another 3 grandchildren.

Steve is an active blogger and social commentator, maintaining a website where he discusses current theological and social issues. If you would like to read more of Steve's work, you can visit his blog using the QR code at right. Simply use a the camera app on your mobile device or computer to navigate there or type in the URL below it.

misc-ramblings.com